HOW TO SET UP AND MANAGE A CORPORATE LEARNING CENTRE

How to set up and manage a corporate learning centre

Second Edition

Samuel A. Malone

Routledge
Taylor & Francis Group

LONDON AND NEW YORK

First published in paperback 2024

First published 2003 by Gower Publishing

Published 2016
by Routledge
4 Park Square, Milton Park, Abingdon, Oxon OX14 4RN

and by Routledge
605 Third Avenue, New York, NY 10158

First Edition published 1997

Routledge is an imprint of the Taylor & Francis Group, an informa business

British Library Cataloguing in Publication Data
Malone, S. A.
  How to set up and manage a corporate learning centre.—2nd ed.
  1. Employer-supported education 2. Employees—Training of
  I. Title
  658.3'124'3

ISBN 13: 978-0-566-08532-1 (hbk)

Library of Congress Cataloging-in-Publication Data
Malone, Samuel A.
  How to set up and manage a corporate learning centre / Samuel A. Malone. —2nd ed.
    p. cm.
  ISBN 0–566–08532–1
  1. Organizational learning—Technological innovations. 2. Open learning—
  Management. 3. Information technology—Management. 4. Employees—Training of.
  5. Educational innovation. I. Title.
  HD58.82.M35 2002
  658.3'12404—dc21   2002035442

ISBN: 978-0-566-08532-1 (hbk)
ISBN: 978-1-03-283757-4 (pbk)
ISBN: 978-1-315-58723-3 (ebk)

DOI: 10.4324/9781315587233

Typeset in 11 point Palatino by Bournemouth Colour Press, Parkstone, Poole, Dorset

Contents

List of figures

xi

Preface

The knowledge acquired in university degrees and professional qualifications rapidly becomes out of date. Many people now change their careers several times during a lifetime. The concept of a job for life is now a thing of the past. To survive and progress in the modern workplace, people must continually update their knowledge and skills. You must adopt the ideas of continuous personal development and lifelong learning to survive in a rapidly changing world.

The modern workplace needs to develop the features of a university, continually developing and learning, if companies are to maintain their competitive edge. The information age has arrived. Information is power. Information is the most valuable and marketable product in the world. Some companies have knowledge management systems to capture this most precious resource. Information provides added value, and differentiates one company from another. With competitive products becoming very similar, companies are differentiating by service and knowledge. Welcome to the information age.

This book will show you how to make education, training, knowledge and skill accessible to everybody in the workplace, irrespective of their formal education, through the use of modern information technology. Today, the PC is becoming as commonplace in the home as the television. The price of hardware and software is now affordable. Every home has the potential to be a corporate learning centre.

The nucleus of a corporate learning centre is already in the home, with television, video recorders, DVD players, the telephone, and the PC with its access to the Internet. Telecommunications technology with cablelink has arrived. In the past few years there has been an explosion in the range and quality of software programmes available in the educational area on audio, CD, video, CD-ROM, DVD, and so on. With Internet-based e-learning programmes, it is now possible to bring advanced education and training programmes right into your own living room. The democratization of education is coming. The barriers to education are falling. Institutions such as the Open University are exploiting modern technology to make university education accessible to those who otherwise could not aspire to it.

Corporate learning centres now supplement 'live' training and on-the-job training in many large companies. This book will show you how to set up and manage a corporate learning centre in your company. It will discuss the motives behind setting up a corporate learning centre and the organizational issues involved in doing so, and alert you to the types of resistance that may be encountered. The management, marketing and administration of a corporate learning centre is discussed in some detail.

S.A. Malone, M Ed MIIE FIITD ACMA ACIS
August 2002

1 Introduction and definitions

The need for open learning

Until the arrival of open, distance and flexible learning, many people were prevented from furthering their education or improving their vocational skills and qualifications. In particular, those with jobs and families were not catered for by conventional tertiary-level education with its constraints of time, prescription, space and cost. Even evening classes require you to attend at a particular time and place and follow regulations designed more for the convenience of the administrators and educators rather than meeting the needs of the adult learner. Many of these courses require formal educational qualifications on entry. Attending courses in outside training establishments presents many of the same kinds of problems. People in rural areas find that training opportunities are almost non-existent. It is only in the large urban centres that you find a broad range of training programmes. This rigidity of timetabling, location and administration can defeat all but the most determined.

The providers of education have been slow to adopt the marketing concept – find out exactly what the customer wants, and then provide the service or product to satisfy that want. The customers in this context are the students, and parents of students. Parent/teacher councils are a step in the right direction. With the arrival of the Open University (OU) and the distance learning degrees of many prestigious universities, this gap in the market is now being filled in the formal educational area. The Open University creates television programmes for the BBC as well as text,

CD-ROMs and audio resources. It has become the model for distance learning programmes throughout the world, with more than 200 000 students in 41 countries.

The advent of new technology such as computer-based training (CBT), e-learning, video and audio, electronic mail (e-mail) and audio and video conferencing means that it has now become feasible for many organizations to bring open learning into the workplace. It is possible to provide training economically on most topics to small groups of employees. Employees were often excluded from training and development opportunities because of lack of variety, flexibility, availability and accessibility of courses. Now training to meet specific needs can be brought right to their doorstep via Internet-based e-learning programmes, and used as and when required.

The purpose and structure of the book

The purpose of this book is to provide you with the information required to set up and manage your own corporate learning centre. This book has eleven chapters. Chapter 1, as well as giving a brief overview of the book, defines open, distance and flexible learning, and shows how the three are incorporated into the concept of corporate learning centres. Corporate learning courses make learning accessible, easy, interactive, self-paced and interesting, and thus combine aspects of open, distance and flexible learning.

Chapter 2 looks at some of the reasons why a company should establish a corporate learning centre. The key benefits of open learning, including accessibility, flexibility, modular structure and continuous feedback, are examined in some detail.

Chapter 3 considers making the most of a corporate learning centre. The importance of identifying training needs, of a good syllabus, and the need to evaluate training are addressed. Some successful corporate learning centres are considered.

Chapter 4 examines the need to establish costs and measure benefits. It will also look at the costs and savings made by various companies which have successfully established corporate learning centres.

Chapter 5 explores the resistance to various types of open learning from managers, trainers and learners, and how to resolve them. The force field model is used to help analyse the factors which help and hinder open learning.

In Chapter 6, the problems and challenges of launching a corporate learning centre are examined. The layout of a typical centre, including the organization of learning booths, is also discussed.

Chapter 7 discusses the media used in corporate learning centres. These include CD-ROM DVD, e-learning, audio, video, CDs, the Internet and e-mail, text-based courses, and magazines and journals. Their strengths and weaknesses are considered.

Chapter 8 looks at the management and administration of a corporate learning centre. A person specification and a job specification for the co-ordinator is considered, as well as the co-ordinator's role and tasks.

Chapter 9 shows you how to market a corporate learning centre. It considers the mission and vision statement, the centre's objective, marketing strategies, objectives and plans, and the need to link these with strategic plans.

Chapter 10 is a learner's guide to using a corporate learning centre. It includes scheduling visits, setting personal objectives, choosing courses, recording progress, and keeping your manager and co-ordinator informed about your plans and progress.

Finally, Chapter 11 draws some conclusions and makes some recommendations for the success of corporate learning centres.

Introduction to distance, flexible and open learning

What is distance learning? What is flexible learning? What is open learning? Do they mean exactly the same thing, or are they three different concepts? In the following sections, we will discuss these issues.

Distance learning

Distance learning takes place at a distance from the preparer and presenter of the learning material. The material should be of a high quality, and be produced with the end user in mind. Correspondence courses were the original distance learning programmes. These were essentially text-based, and were widely used by the accountancy and other business professions. For nearly a hundred years, correspondence colleges have been preparing accountancy students to qualify as professional members of the various accountancy bodies and other business institutes such as the Institute of Chartered Secretaries and Administrators and the Chartered Institute of Personnel and Development. These colleges gave people the opportunity to qualify as professionals by self-study without attending educational establishments.

The institutes set examinations and standards, but do not concern themselves with the mode of preparation. This process is left to the discretion of the student, and is very flexible. Thus many trainee accountants, who work during the day and spend many nights away from their home base on audit assignments, study accountancy through a correspondence course in their own time, but often with the financial support of the employer. Handy (1988) sees this approach to open learning as the way forward in the future:

> The kind of management training system that I see is one modelled on our professions like accountancy. Every would be manager, be he or she engineer, chemist, computer expert or whatever, should have done some homework and learn the language of his or her profession before he or she is more than two or three years in the job. That can be readily and easily done through that delivery system that we are so great at: open learning supported by company-based mentors.

The Japanese use the correspondence course as a cost-effective method to upgrade executive skills in business and management theory. As Hardy (1988) points out: 'Self-enlightenment is Japanese for correspondence courses.'

The text in correspondence school courses these days has in many cases been supplemented by audio, video, CD-ROM, DVD and, of course, books. Some certificate, diploma and degree programmes are now delivered exclusively through e-learning on the Internet. E-learning is a type of distance learning, and uses the Internet or an intranet as a delivery system. Distance learning, unlike correspondence courses, may be supported by e-learning modules and residential courses which give learners the opportunity to meet others and seek tutors' guidance in workshops, on the telephone, or through online mentoring.

In response to market demand, distance learning has now been adopted by many of the major universities. The leaders in this field are the Open University and the University for Industry (UfI). The term *learndirect* is the brand name for UfI. Adult learners may now acquire certificate, diploma, primary degrees, masters degrees and qualifications up to PhD level through this medium. The majority of distance and online programmes currently on the market focus on courses paid for by businesses or which clearly improve an individual's job prospects. For example, IBM sponsors its executives on OU MBA courses. Freathy (1991) describes a distance learning MBA in retailing and wholesaling run by Stirling University. Johnston (1993) says that evidence from Sheffield University's distance learning masters degree in Training and Development suggests a high level of satisfaction with this method of continuing professional development from participants and sponsoring companies. As of 2002, NETg, through Cardean University in the USA, offers a flexible MBA programme online. Busy professionals are given the opportunity to obtain a masters degree while continuing to work.

Distance learning can be integrated with the facilities and programmes of the corporate learning centre, which means that employees engaged in distance learning programmes can use the courseware and e-learning programmes of the corporate learning centres to help them in their studies as well as in their jobs. Some professional bodies, such as the Institute of Bankers, the Accountancy Institutes and the CIPD, have produced complete subject programmes for their examinations using the computer-based training media, including e-learning programmes that can be accessed in corporate learning centres. Corporate learning centres can be linked up to educational establishments in order to obtain certification or national vocational qualifications for their courses. They can also subscribe to recognized e-learning programmes online, such as the European Computer Driving Licence (ECDL).

Birchall (1990) introduces the idea of third-generation distance learning. He says the approach adopted in the early 1980s may be considered second-generation distance learning, first-generation being traditional correspondence education. Students use various media – mostly audio, video, CD-ROM/DVD and text-based. In addition, they are offered 'support services', comprising a helpline and tutor-led workshops. This type of service can be provided by corporate learning centres.

Third-generation distance learning aims to overcome the lack of interaction and the problems of isolation experienced by many distance learners. It gives the student access to others from the workplace or home. The Internet, audio and video conferencing and e-mail are being used for remote teaching. E-mail can be used for transmission of information direct to the home, and can also be used for conferencing. Both facilities offer scope for two-way communication, and give a new dimension to education. Voice mail means that your tutor can offer guidance and advice even when you're not at home. The Internet offers real-time collaboration with a network of mentors, experts and fellow learners.

Flexible learning

'Flexible learning' is a term used to describe both open and distance learning. In practice, the three terms open, distance and flexible learning are often used interchangeably, but there may be subtle differences between these approaches. Van den Brande (1993) defines flexible learning as follows:

> Flexible learning is enabling learners to learn when they want (frequency, timing, duration), how they want (modes of learning), and what they want (that is learners can define what constitutes learning to them). These flexible learning principles may be applied at a distance. If so then the term 'distance learning' is used. In such cases the learners can choose where they want to learn (at home, at an institution or company, at a training centre, etc.).

In addition, throughout the world, open, distance and flexible learning are defined in a variety of ways. These are not merely the result of different languages and culture, but rather the outcome of different educational, training and vocational training systems and alternative applications of new technology. Thus the term *Fernunterricht* ('distance education') is used in Germany, 'open learning' in the UK, and *Formation Multimedia* in France.

Open learning

The term 'open learning' suggests that no pre-qualifications are necessary to take part in the programme, such as age, status or formal examinations. It also suggests flexibility in deciding where to learn (such as at home), when to learn (such as in the morning, at lunchtime or in the evening), how to learn (through delivery systems such as text, CD-ROM, DVD, the Internet, audio and video), and the pace at which to learn, which is decided by the adult learner. In practice, many open learning programmes run by educational or training establishments may set minimum academic standards and other criteria for admission.

A corporate learning centre is just one application of the concept of open learning, and is the principal focus of this book. Other applications would be correspondence schools, the Open University and virtual learning centres based on company intranets. In a corporate learning centre, learning is made accessible to all staff who want to learn and go on learning. It's a type of industrial democracy in action, providing learner empowerment. The emphasis is on continuous learning and improvement throughout an employee's career.

Corporate learning centre courses make learning accessible, easy, self-paced and interesting. The courses are designed around different forms of media. They range from text-based, audio and video tapes to CD-ROM, DVD, the Internet and e-mail. However, unlike conventional learning that is teacher-centred, the responsibility for open learning lies with the learner.

In this book, the term 'corporate learning centres' combines aspects of the three ideas of open learning, distance and flexible learning. This concept is shown in Figure 1.1.

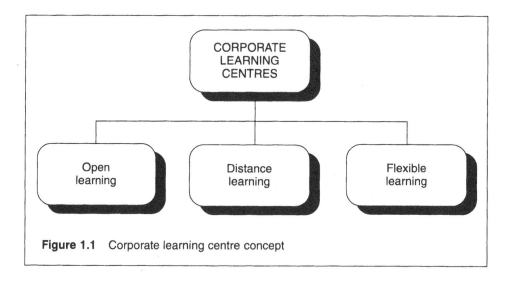

Figure 1.1   Corporate learning centre concept

Corporate learning centres are open because any employee may make use of their services without regard to grade, gender, age, disability, qualifications and so on. In addition, employees who take part in the distance learning programmes of the major universities and professional bodies may use open learning centres' facilities to prepare for examinations. In fact, complete subject areas are now available via Internet-based e-learning programmes or on CD-ROM/DVD, and there are a vast number of topical academic areas on audio and video.

For example, the BBC, Open University, Video Arts, Fenman and Gower, among others, have shown what can be achieved producing high-quality audio and video programmes aimed at tertiary-level and professional students, many of which are in corporate learning centres. Where an organization is geographically scattered through a branch network, the centre's services may be accessed through wide area networks (WANs). In addition, Internet access provides a huge range of e-learning programmes. NETg and SmartForce are among the leading suppliers offering a comprehensive range of e-learning programmes which can be accessed online in corporate learning centres. Corporate learning centres offer flexible learning, in that learners may learn what they want when they want, and how they want.

Traditional training versus corporate learning centre training

Traditional training is carried out in groups and to a fixed schedule, although the style and pace of delivery is influenced by the group. There may be a fear of exposure or failure on the part of the trainee. The training tends to be interactive, but specific to the training needs of the trainees. Corporate learning centre training, on the other hand, is conducted individually (although working in pairs is sometimes recommended, and collaborative learning is a feature of e-learning), and delivery is flexible, in that the learner can skip ahead or move back and repeat a module if necessary. The pace of delivery is determined by the user. The corporate learning centre is managed by a generalist co-ordinator, and the learning environment is seen as non-threatening. There is limited interaction, and programmes are generic in nature, in that they are designed for mass audiences. A summary comparison is shown in Figure 1.2.

Summary

Distance learning takes place at a distance from those who prepare and present the learning material. Correspondence courses were the original distance learning programmes. E-learning is a modern version of distance learning. 'Flexible learning' is a term used to describe both open and

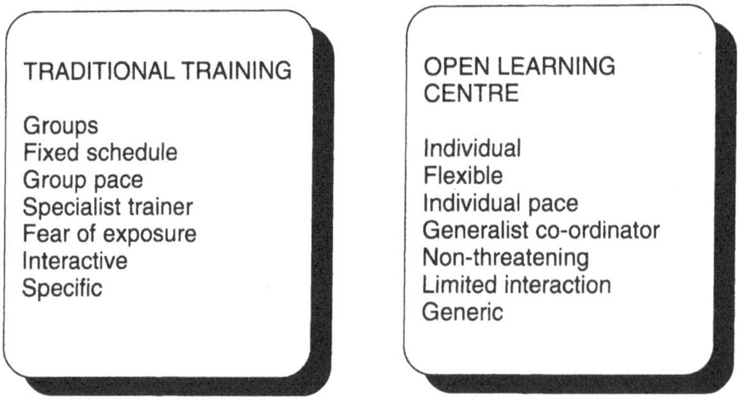

TRADITIONAL TRAINING

Groups
Fixed schedule
Group pace
Specialist trainer
Fear of exposure
Interactive
Specific

OPEN LEARNING
CENTRE

Individual
Flexible
Individual pace
Generalist co-ordinator
Non-threatening
Limited interaction
Generic

Figure 1.2   Comparison of traditional and corporate learning centre training

distance learning. Flexible learning enables people to learn what they want when they want and where they want.

Open learning suggests that no pre-qualifications are necessary to take part in the programmes, such as age, status or formal examinations. A corporate learning centre is just one application of the concept of open learning. Corporate learning centre courses make learning accessible, easy, self-paced and interesting. They combine aspects of the three ideas of open learning, distance learning and flexible learning.

2 Why establish a corporate learning centre?

Introduction

Corporate learning centres are designed to:

1. meet identified training and business needs
2. increase productivity and cost-effectiveness by improving employees' on-the-job performance and their ability to cope with change, developments in technology, or by equipping them to take on extra responsibility.
3. create a learning culture throughout the organization.

The success of the centre will be reflected in improved job satisfaction, better morale, greater efficiency, increased sales, improved customer service, increased quality, reduced costs and greater profits.

Knowledge-based added value is the key competitive advantage of any company. Most studies suggest that properly managed open learning is more cost-effective than traditional methods of training, and enables employees to learn faster and retain more. This is particularly true where large numbers need to be trained in standardized procedures, or small numbers need to be trained in dangerous procedures or the use of expensive equipment.

The motives for introducing corporate learning centres include a desire to keep up to date with information technology, facilitating the learning organization ethos, and making provision for continuing professional education and lifelong learning. The key benefits of open learning are as follows:

- It recognizes the fact that different people learn at different speeds and in different ways.
- It is an active form of learning.
- It helps individuals accept responsibility for their own learning.
- It helps people learn how to learn.
- It encourages self-motivation, and dispels the idea that attendance on courses is the equivalent of effort and achievement.

In addition, rising standards of computer literacy, the increased sophistication of PC technology, improved telecommunications systems including the Internet, the greater variety of software available and falling costs in both software and hardware have all helped the process along.

The information technology revolution

In the last few years there has been a gradual move away from total reliance on a tutor-centred approach to a more student-centred and self-reliant approach. Organizationally, there has been a move away from central control of training to decentralization and learner empowerment. In a competitive situation, with a need to reduce costs, training and development is often seen as a non-core activity. There are constant pressures on management to reduce the training budget or get more value from the training investment. Consequently, in times of recession training is often the first business activity to be cut back. Decentralization of training and reductions in training costs can now be achieved with the application of computer-based technology, including Internet-based e-learning. In addition, a company may feel that it has fallen behind in the rapidly changing information technology scene. As a result, it may need to bring large numbers of its staff up to speed in the latest information technology quickly and cost-effectively.

The logistics of providing 'live' courses in information technology – or indeed any subject – to large numbers of employees are formidable. This could be addressed by getting staff to do it themselves more cost-effectively in corporate learning centres. In fact, corporate learning centres are particularly suited for information technology skills, and the quality and range of CD-ROM/DVD and e-learning programmes now available in this area are impressive.

Computer literacy skills are just as important in business as the more conventional skills of reading, writing and arithmetic. Familiarity with computerized corporate systems and the better-known desktop publishing, word processing, spreadsheet and graphics software packages is now considered essential for many jobs. In the new information age, everybody should have some familiarity with computers.

The use of different media in the corporate learning centre will also develop new competencies in staff through familiarization with audio, video, CD-ROM/DVD, the Internet and e-mail, and the hands-on approach to computer hardware. People's fears about using computers are quickly overcome. In any event, the helpful tutorial skills and friendly guidance of the learning centre co-ordinator are always on hand when needed. In addition, e-learning programmes are more collaborative, with online mentoring and tutorial help. More importantly, the corporate learning centre gives people a resource that they can use to help solve work-related problems.

The learning organization

Most organizations want to be seen as modern, progressive and go-ahead Corporate learning centres are a relatively new and inexpensive approach to the delivery of training. If you want to maintain your competitive advantage, you need to keep up with improvements in information technology. More importantly, your staff must have the expertise to use the information technology effectively. This expertise can now be self-taught in corporate learning centres. Firms also want to be seen to be doing something concrete to demonstrate their commitment to become a learning organization and support the concept of lifelong continuous learning and learner empowerment.

Many experts claim that the Japanese maintain their competitive edge through their considerable investment in training. Surveys show that Britain and Ireland fall badly behind in investment in training compared with other EU countries such as Germany (which is renowned for its training culture), the USA and Japan. Open learning is now seen as a practical, cost-effective and democratic method to train, educate, develop and empower staff, and an efficient way to bridge the training gap.

In the West, we must move away from Taylor's scientific management approach that the boss knows best and has a monopoly on knowledge. Under this approach, the planning and control of work is seen as the manager's responsibility. The manager designs the work methods, and workers are meant to do what they are told. It is the conventional command and control approach. Thus workers are seen as brawn rather than brain. Modern management thinking suggests workers should have a say in work design, and should take responsibility for their own learning. Therefore, we need to encourage employees to use their intelligence and creativity to improve work methods and processes and to become more self-reliant.

With its use of modern technology, the corporate learning centre exposes learners to the latest developments in information technology. Keyboarding, PC and Internet familiarization programmes are available for novices to help them get started. For more advanced learners, there are CD-ROM/DVD and e-learning programmes available on all the major software packages, including *Microsoft Windows*. People using the CD-ROM/DVD and e-learning programmes in many cases find them as good as the equivalent live courses, and more flexible and cost-effective. The CD-ROM/DVD and e-learning programmes offer the added advantage of self-pacing, allowing repeated practice as required.

Open learning underpins the knowledge-based society

Corporate learning centres, through the application of educational technology, use a different delivery system to meet training and development needs. Open learning should be seen as complementary to conventional training, rather than a substitute for it. Waterhouse (1990) suggests that it equips people for the demands of working life in a rapidly changing, highly technological society. Computer-based training, including e-learning, is now capable of delivering a wide variety of quality training programmes which a well-staffed conventional training department could not match. In fact, *blended learning* is now considered the best way forward. This term describes a process that matches the exact learning needs and preferred learning style of the individual to a range of content and training techniques such as e-learning, online mentoring, instructor-led training, on-the-job training, books, videos, audios, CDs, and CD-ROM/DVDs. It has been estimated that the knowledge base of society is now doubling every seven years. In the modern world, most people will change jobs and pursue different careers during a lifetime. The day of the lifetime permanent pensionable job has gone. It is therefore, essential that everyone be willing to upgrade their existing skills and able to learn new skills as necessary. Basic computer skills are now essential to survive in the workplace. Internet-based e-learning programmes and knowledge management systems will allow many more people access to the information they need. The most critical life skills are now considered to be learning-to-learn skills, and the ability to go on learning. It is the intellectual capital, or the totality of what employees know, which gives a company a competitive advantage.

Continuing professional education

A number of professional bodies, including accounting, engineering and personnel institutes, now require their members to upgrade their skills each year. In the modern, rapidly changing world, knowledge and skills quickly become out of date. Engineers, accountants and technicians now realize that their knowledge base will quickly become obsolete unless they take positive action to keep up to date. Professional knowledge is likely to be outmoded within five years unless updated. In particular, e-learning facilitates personal growth and professional development.

Professions recognize the need for lifelong learning. Some of the programmes stocked in the corporate learning centre and e-learning programmes meet the institutes' requirements for continuing professional education. This saves on the cost of employee attendance at outside courses, which can be quite expensive for companies to support. The certification of corporate learning centre courses can be arranged with local educational institutes.

Key benefits of open learning

Harper (1993) summarizes the case for open learning from the learner's perspective as follows. It:

- recognizes that different students learn at different speeds and in different ways;
- helps students to be more active in their learning;
- helps students to accept greater responsibility for their own learning;
- helps students to learn how to learn;
- generates motivation and commitment and stimulates a sense of self-management;
- dispels the student idea that attendance in class is equivalent to effort and achievement.

People learn at different speeds and in different ways

In a 'live' training course, the trainer's presentation is aimed at a common denominator of participants' experience, knowledge and ability, so that individual variations in learning ability and prior knowledge are not catered for. For example, a learner may have to sit through a whole course just to get a small piece of relevant information. In computer-based training (CBT), you can go directly to the information you need. Repetition and practice is a key principle of learning, and one that open learning courses facilitate. Trainees can go back over different areas as often as necessary until the relevant skill or knowledge base is acquired. In 'live' training, this is not practicable. Using computer courseware or e-learning programmes, you can be sure that the same standard programme is provided for each trainee whereas in live training variations will occur due to changes in delivery and mood and the receptiveness of the learner.

CBT caters for different learning styles. Research into how people learn and remember suggests that we retain about 20 per cent of what we hear, 40 per cent of what we see and hear, and 75 per cent of what we see, hear and do. Multimedia engages all the senses – hearing, seeing and doing – and thus maximizes learning while catering for every learning style.

Comparative studies suggest that learning effectiveness of CBT is superior to conventional training – people learn faster, and retain more. Some studies have shown an improvement in the time required to learn of 50 per cent. This is due to:

- **Self-pacing** – because the learning is self-paced, the learner can take the most efficient path to learn the content.
- **Interaction and feedback** – the courseware is specially designed to provide reinforcement by giving plenty of practice. In some courses, learners are now allowed to progress until earlier stages have been mastered.

More focused and active learning

In a corporate learning centre course, people can focus on exactly the area they want to develop. Peripheral areas can be ignored. They can concentrate on the issues that are currently relevant to their needs. They can move back, fast-forward, skip, stop, repeat and exit as they please.

With the rapid advances in information technology, the shortcomings of programmed learning on cumbersome teaching machines have been largely overcome. In fact, the best of learning theory has now been successfully incorporated into the design of CBT programmes to help people learn enjoyably, quickly and effectively. Fricker (1988) maintains that open learning courses should be user-friendly, and the content and style should be practical and visually good, and facilitate active learning.

Learner responsibility

Temple (1988) maintains that enterprising, self-starting and self-directing people are what companies need. In a fast-changing and competitive environment, companies need to develop staff with self-reliance and initiative, and who are keen to learn and equip themselves with new skills. The philosophy that managers have a monopoly on brainpower, ideas and knowledge is becoming outmoded. The creativity and knowledge of the workforce should be engaged. The development of intellectual capital must be encouraged and nurtured.

Open learning is an ideal means of developing the necessary skills and attitudes of self-reliance and initiative, precisely because they are exactly those which are acquired when doing open learning. Staff who are self-reliant do not wait around to be told what to learn. They identify their own training needs, draw up their own personal development plans, and then set about meeting those needs themselves. Open learning provides the means to do this. In practice, some people may not be self-motivated, self-disciplined and capable of taking responsibility for their own learning. These people need the traditional training approach, with a trainer for encouragement and direction. They also need the encouragement and guidance of managers to undertake training.

Helping learners to learn

A feature of CBT and e-learning is the interaction and continuous feedback and evaluation of performance. The principles of programmed learning are used in the design of courses. The whole emphasis of CBT and e-learning is on helping learners to learn effectively. Information is presented in chunks, with associated questions to test understanding – the stimulus–response–reinforcement principle. Learners do not move ahead until the relevant skill or knowledge has been mastered. There is a gradual acquisition of skill and expertise with little chance of information overload. Because of the proximity of the workplace, staff can immediately apply the skills and knowledge learned in the actual work situation.

Feedback is an important principle in learning, and is automatically built in to well-designed, high-quality learning courses. Some do not allow you to progress until you have dealt with the previous section satisfactorily. More formal assessment may also be a feature of open learning programmes. These could take the form of examinations, questionnaires or progress tests.

Motivation

The availability of a corporate learning centre in a company can boost staff morale and motivation. It is a visible demonstration that the company cares about the development of its employees. Learners are made autonomous, and encouraged to identify and meet their own training needs as and when required. They draw up their own personal development plans, set their own learning objectives, and become responsible for their own learning, and thus feel a sense of empowerment. As Coldeway (1982) points out, this is in line with modern educational theory and management thinking.

To attract learners, the training experience provided by the corporate learning centre must give employees an opportunity to develop competencies directly relevant to their jobs. The training must be perceived as useful for career progression and promotion inside or outside the company. Using the corporate learning centre must have status and acceptability with the employees' peer group. These factors will affect the motivation of learners.

Attendance does not mean effort and achievement

Attendance at a 'live' course does not necessarily mean that people are learning. Some individuals are nominated by their managers to attend training courses, sometimes against their own wishes. In such circumstances, they will have little commitment to the training. Other people are sent on courses for the wrong reasons – as a reward for good · job performance or for rest and recreation. Such individuals are also unlikely to be committed to the training. In any case, it is easier to daydream and lose concentration in a 'live' training situation than when pursuing a corporate learning centre course, because of the greater degree of feedback involved in open learning courseware.

Accessibility of time and place

Barriers to traditional training often exist because of lack of accessibility. This may be due to lack of availability of courses, or distance, domestic and work-related constraints. Corporate learning centres bring training directly to the user at a convenient time and place, using top-quality and proven course material, including a wide range of Internet-based e-learning programmes. *Business Wire* (17 April 2000) reported that the Gates Rubber Company in the USA uses the click2learn.com corporate e-learning site with pay-as-you-go access to thousands of Web-based courses, books and CD-ROMs on information technology and general business topics. The new e-learning site is configured to fit Gates' Website design and navigation standards, and is integrated with the existing employee intranet.

Flexibility

Staff can pursue open learning courses at their own pace, in their own time, and without supervision, threat or fear of competition. Lunchtime, before or after normal working hours, weekends and any time during work allowed by their managers may be suitable. Shift workers can make use of learning opportunities that would not normally be available to them because of the unsociable hours they work. Courses can be studied as often as needed, and complicated topics repeated as necessary.

Training is provided all year round, on demand which is not possible in a live training situation. In addition, many educational and training establishments close down for summer, Christmas and Easter vacations. Disruption of work is minimized, travelling time and accommodation costs are eliminated. People become more flexible in their attitudes to new methods and new technology, especially in the acceptance of change through continuous lifelong learning. The 'drop in and help yourself to learning' approach creates an ethos and culture of learning in the individual and in the organization. The barriers to learning are eliminated when it becomes available to all employees.

One of the big advantages of a corporate learning centre is that staff with some spare time, can make use of the opportunity there and then to upgrade their knowledge and skills, instead of wasting time attending an internal or external 'live' course at a set time which may not suit them.

Equality

There are many barriers which prevent staff from taking up training and development opportunities. Some people find it difficult to attend courses held centrally in headquarters, which entails travel and being away overnight, because of family commitments. Part-time workers, temporary staff and job sharers are often excluded from traditional training and development courses. The courses in a corporate learning centre are more accessible. Open learning is seen as a means of meeting their needs without disruption of work, travelling time and overnight stays.

Research studies show that older staff tend to learn more slowly than younger staff, and that there is a small decline in their working memory. Older staff are often reluctant to go on 'live' training programmes because of fear of not being able to keep up and of looking foolish in front of their younger colleagues. The privacy and self-pacing of the corporate learning centre approach overcomes this problem. Older learners find computer-based training to be of special advantage because they can control the pace of their work, the amount of revision devoted to difficult issues, and the ways in which they can explore and test out new concepts. A corporate learning centre will provide the facilities for life-long learning irrespective of age and the opportunities for personal development and perhaps career advancement.

It is good company policy that learning opportunities should be provided on a democratic basis for a greater range and number of employees. The corporate learning centre provides this opportunity, and puts the onus for learning on the learner – where it should be. The learner's requirement is the commitment to learn expressed in the form of time, willpower, persistence, dedication and application. Learning is hard work. It requires pain and sacrifice in the present in return for future gain.

Maintaining competitive advantage

Specific training needs should be integrated into individual training plans and work programmes derived from annual business plans and the strategic objective. The idea of continuous improvement is essential if a business is to prosper and survive. Continuous improvements in product design, manufacturing process, customer service, organization structure, information technology and telecommunications means that employees must frequently update their knowledge and skills. The modern workplace needs to become more and more like the learning community of a university. In fact, some companies such as Motorola have set up their own corporate universities. Corporate learning centres, like corporate universities, should be a visible underpinning of the philosophy of the learning organization and the concept of lifelong learning, training and development. Prickett (2002) maintains that employers may have to invest more in e-learning technology in the future if they are to keep up with increasingly well-informed clients. E-training for customers has arrived. Charles Schwab, for example, provides online share-dealing services, and is offering subscribers e-lessons about investing.

Modular basis

Corporate learning centre courses are organized on a modular basis. Remember that the length of a module should be reasonably short in order to avoid demotivating people. A journey of a thousand miles begins with a single step. People are motivated to learn by concentrating on learning objectives supported by achievable and manageable chunks of materials. Reinforcement and reward should be a feature of each step.

The modular design of courses also facilitates use as and when staff have the available time, which in practice can be in half-hour blocks. In fact, since the average attention span is about 20 minutes, half-hour study sessions are just about the ideal length to maximize concentration and learning. To maintain concentration, learners should be advised to take five-minute breaks every hour, and two-minute breaks every 20 minutes. Open learning not only gives the learner power to define when and over what period they learn and when to take breaks, but also the content and form the learning should take.

With the modular structure of most courseware, learners can use the menu to go to the particular topic they want. Thus there is no need to go through information that you know already, and learning is speeded up.

Miller, a psychologist, discovered the '7 plus or minus 2' rule in memory, which suggests that people have difficulty learning more than nine items at a time. Modular design on this basis would suggest that courseware should contain not more than nine modules, each module with not more than nine sections, and each section containing not more than nine points. This is important to keep in mind in the design or selection of courseware. The modular design enables people to move around the programme quickly without having to stick to a rigid sequence. It also helps them to find the particular information they need. A good menu will facilitate the process.

Greater quality control

The quality and relevance of corporate learning courseware can be tested and judged in advance. Consistency of presentation, which is not possible with traditional training, is assured. Deciding whether to send somebody on an external course is often determined by a glossy brochure rather than proper validation.

The quality of course materials used in open learning will be consistent and not subject to an 'off day' on the trainer's part. Trainers are released from routine training so that they can concentrate on the more demanding, urgent and specific needs of their organization. The standard of courseware has improved considerably over the years, and the range and quality of software and e-learning programmes is good. Choose the best material available for your corporate learning centre.

Most programmes are now designed in line with the best educational and learning principles. Open learning courseware is piloted extensively before launch by the vendors. Feedback is collected from a sample of learners via questionnaires, interviews and so on. Modifications are made based on the feedback obtained. Because of the known costs, budgets should be easier to compile, control and manage. Learning management systems are sophisticated, facilitating the administration, control and evaluation of programmes.

Simulations

Multimedia courseware enables employees to explore safely the operation of expensive and potentially dangerous equipment in a risk-free environment. For example, many armies use computer-based simulation technology to train soldiers. On-the-job safety routines can also be learnt, such as power station operation simulators for the training of power workers, and flight simulators for training pilots. Lavitt (1995), for example, reports than an Israeli company is offering a multimedia aircraft recognition training system that can be used for all phases of training of pilots, aircrews and intelligence personnel. The sophistication of simulators has been enhanced with the development of virtual reality, and the potential applications of this new technology are enormous.

Shepherd (2001a) reports that business-modelling simulations are used in subjects such as finance and accounting. They allow students to manipulate a wide variety of financial variables in a virtual company, and learn how these variables interact.

Safety, health and welfare programmes are now available on video, CD-ROM/DVD and Internet-based e-learning. Some companies produce their own videos in this area which deal specifically with their country's legislation and specific organizational requirements. Remember there is a statutory requirement that a company comply with safety legislation and that employees receive proper instruction in safety procedures. E-learning is particularly suited to compliance and regulatory-type subjects such as health and safety and accounting.

Job aids

Job aids can provide just-in-time training via the Internet or intranet. Job aids may be resident on the computer as a form of on-the-job training or a knowledge management system to be used as and when required. Many skills are learned and retained more effectively when there is an immediate need to learn and apply them. Give training too early, and learners will forget. Give training too late, and learners will have already learned by trial and error, giving rise to inappropriate and inefficient work methods.

Job aids can be used instead of cumbersome procedural manuals, detailed work guides or seeking assistance from your supervisor. Ganger (1994) reports that in a typical bank job aid system, employees use a desktop computer when a customer requests any of a dozen relatively complicated bank services. The employee enters the type of transaction, and the job aid program produces a listing of all forms needed, where to locate them, and the procedures that must be performed. Obviously, with the passage of time the user will become less reliant on the system to identify forms and procedures, and become more self-sufficient.

Shepherd (2001b) reports on the development of learning objects as part of knowledge management systems. He maintains that there is a growing interest in *learning objects* – small self-contained modules of content delivered just in time to aid learning. Learners need a help screen when using a computer application, or a few Web pages when they need specific guidance. Much on-the-job learning will take place in two- or three-minute chunks, not two- or three-day courses.

No panacea for all training needs

Open learning is unlikely to be a panacea for all training needs. Computer-based training is highly appropriate for technical topics such as accountancy, information technology and engineering. A significant number of training departments now use CBT to teach computer-related skills as well as other technical skills. However, some areas such as the 'soft' skills are better dealt with by other methods, including traditional educational and training courses and on-the-job training.

For example, you could learn all about the theory of driving a car from watching a video or taking a computer-based course, but you would still be unable to drive the car. You need to acquire practical competencies to drive, which you can only acquire by driving. Obviously, skill-based training is facilitated best through live demonstrations, frequent practice and immediate feedback.

For business and management subjects, you can pick up the theory from CBT and e-learning programmes, but this needs to be supported by on-the-job experience if you want to acquire real understanding and practical expertise. The theory of public speaking can be learned in an open learning centre course, but the practical skills can only be acquired in a 'live' programme. Similarly, you could learn all about the theory of writing by working through a computer-based programme, but you still need practice and 'live' coaching in writing skills.

Kattackal (1994) reports that:

> CBT represents only one piece of the training puzzle. It should not be chosen in isolation, but rather it should be linked to other training efforts, including on-the-job training. A new staff member can learn about the audit process by having the computer present audit concepts, methods, and techniques via CBT. However, this type of training in isolation will not produce a competent auditor.
>
> The development of presentation and writing skills, interviewing techniques, and analytical skills are just some of the complex topics that cannot be readily taught using a software program ... at least, not yet. In general, CBT is a clear choice for learning software applications; but, so far, it's not particularly effective at imparting audit skills.

Stephenson (1992) found that even with computer-based training, the presence of a tutor improves performance: 'There is simply something about having another human around and aware of your actions that alters your behaviour.' A study in 2002 by the Thompson Corporation, NETg's parent company, shows that e-learning is most effective when it forms part of a blended programme, typically incorporating online content and simulations, online mentoring and instructor-led training.

There is a danger that setting up a corporate learning centre may be seen as an aim in itself, rather than focusing on its effects. Although the technology looks impressive, it should be seen as just another way to deliver training. In fact, in some companies corporate learning centres have not been successful and have been closed down largely due to failure to identify real business needs, plus inadequate planning, poor marketing and lack of management and employee support. A corporate learning centre offers a cost-effective alternative to some traditional forms of training. If this is unlikely to be the case in your organization, then don't make the investment.

Summary

In the last few years there has been a gradual move away from total reliance on a tutor-centred approach to a more student-centred and self-reliant approach. Rising standards of computer literacy, the increased sophistication of PC technology, improved telecommunications systems, Internet access, the growth of e-learning and knowledge management systems, the greater variety of software available and falling costs of hardware and software have all helped this process along. The need to empower employees and the need to create a learning organization culture have been other motivators for corporate learning centres.

The key benefits of open learning are as follows:

- It caters for people who learn at different speeds and in different ways.
- It encourages active learning.
- It helps individuals accept responsibility for their own learning.
- It helps students learn how to learn.
- It generates motivation and commitment.
- It dispels the idea that attendance in class is equivalent to effort and achievement.

The other benefits of open learning include:

- accessibility of time and place
- greater flexibility
- facilitating equality of opportunity
- helping to maintain or create competitive advantage
- modular design for more focused use
- greater control over quality of training
- simulating safety procedures
- providing job aids and just-in-time learning.

Open learning is not a panacea for all training needs. Some training needs are more appropriately met by 'live' training courses or a blended approach to learning.

3 Making the most of a corporate learning centre

Introduction

When considering how to make the most of a learning centre, the main issues involve:

- identifying training needs
- drawing up a relevant syllabus in response to those needs
- evaluating training

Only the most job-relevant and best-quality courseware and e-learning programmes should be chosen for the centre. A good learning management system will be needed for training records, general administration, control and evaluation. It is important that the centre has the support of management, and that access for staff is made easy.

Identified training needs

As part of the annual business planning process, managers should go through the individual training plans with their staff and identify training necessary to their work programmes. Managers should consider whether the corporate learning centre can meet their needs before sending their staff to the internal training centre or external training establishments. Corporate learning centre courses may prove more cost-effective. A detailed course catalogue should be provided for each manager or displayed on the corporate intranet. By studying the catalogue, they can decide to what extent their training needs can be met by corporate learning centre courses.

The section work programmes are tied to annual business plans, which in turn are linked to the strategic objectives, so that training is now part of the corporate planning process. Because staff are involved in drawing up individual training plans, they are likely to be more committed to them, and more motivated to implement them. The participation of employees in drawing up personal development plans is an example of empowerment in action.

Open learning should be specifically targeted towards an identified training need. It should be used to complement other training methods, as it is unlikely to be an appropriate solution for *all* training needs. Managers should ensure that the corporate learning centre courses are relevant to their employee's current and future job needs, or to their personal development and the needs of the organization. Learners should be encouraged to reflect on how the knowledge and skills gained can be applied to their jobs.

Syllabus

The style and content of the syllabus will need to reflect personal and organizational aims, real training and business needs, and the culture of the organization, and tie in with existing training programmes. If the organization needs to improve information technology skills, this will be apparent from the number of such courses on offer in the syllabus, and similiar observations apply if the company has a big commitment to the personal development needs of staff. Employees who wish to study certificate, diploma and degree programmes to qualify should be offered a range of relevant academic course material. Many colleges now meet this need through Internet-based e-learning programmes accessible from the corporate learning centre. Any company that wishes to become more marketing-orientated in its business approach will reflect this desire in the number of marketing and customer relations-type courses available in the centre or offered through Internet-based e-learning programmes.

The syllabus should be published in two formats – a pocket-size users' handbook to serve as a guide to corporate learning centre courses for learners, and a detailed course catalogue for managers. These should also be made available on the intranet.

Evaluation

Evaluation is the assessment of the total value of a training course in behavioural and financial terms. In other words: has the trainee acquired the required skills or knowledge, and is the training good value for money? Basically, one needs to evaluate at four levels:

1. What are the opinion and attitudes of trainees to the learning experience?
2. What new knowledge, skills, attitudes and behaviours have they learnt?
3. Have they applied this knowledge, skills, attitudes and behaviours to their jobs?
4. Has the efficiency, effectiveness and profitability of the company been improved as a direct result?

It is important that learners who use the corporate learning centre should complete end-of-course evaluation sheets. These can be used to monitor the quality, acceptability and relevance of course programmes. In addition, individual learners and their supervisors should be followed up after a time to gain a picture of the effectiveness of a particular package and the value of the centre as a learning resource. The following information should be established:

- Did the course meet the learner's expectations, and was the learner able to apply the knowledge and skill acquired in the workplace?
- Was there a noticeable improvement in performance as a result? Results may be evaluated at the departmental or corporate level by cost benefit analysis.
- What financial savings and other benefits are attributable directly to the course, and are these greater than the cost of running the programme?

The information obtained from this continuous evaluation can be used to improve the services of the corporate learning centre and make the programmes more focused.

Certification by outside bodies

Certification should be sought for certain programmes initially, and extended to all courses if successful. It is an added attraction if courses are certified by an outside, independent tertiary-level college. For example, the corporate learning centre could be used to support staff studying for the City and Guilds Certificate in Information Technology and Business Skills. Linking up corporate learning centre courses with suitable distance learning programmes of tertiary-level colleges at certificate, diploma and degree level is also a possibility. In fact, co-operative joint ventures between corporate learning centres and colleges should be encouraged.

Training Journal (July 1999) reports that Britannia Building Society recently launched a staff training facility for its 4000 employees nationwide with an online link to Stoke-on-Trent College. Britannia's learning centre will give staff full access to the college's training network and Britannia's own training materials. It will provide development on anything from management skills to learning French.

The British Computer Society administers the ECDL scheme, and accredits organizations which provide the training. In addition, you can prepare for the BCS professional exams using online training. Many high-tech companies such as Microsoft have developed online certification programmes. Being a Microsoft-certified technician or engineer is a general entry-level qualification in the ICT fields.

Singer (2000) reports that the University of Maryland University College in the USA, using Internet learning, offers 26 full degree programmes, 14 undergraduate, including accounting, communications and management, and 12 graduate programmes, which are more focused on management. There are also 40 certificate programmes. Students from 29 countries are enrolled on courses. The University of Michigan Business School has partnered with FT Knowledge to offer no-credit programmes aimed at middle managers, including sales management, marketing, and financial management, at about $3000 per course.

Dunn (2001) reports that European business schools are starting to follow the US model and adopt e-learning for their MBA programmes. In the UK, FT Knowledge has an alliance with Cambridge University to create an E-MBA. Hills (2002) points out that the CIPD provides a range of certificate courses delivered flexibly including a completely online Certificate in Online Learning. The Virtual College provides courses leading to Level 2 NVQs in a variety of technical subjects.

Courseware programmes

Validation

Before purchasing courseware or subscribing to e-learning programmes, they should be validated by subject matter experts for:

- quality
- relevance
- user-friendliness
- learning-effectiveness
- accessibility to learners
- value for money.

Subject matter experts might be staff employed in functional areas or specialist positions. Programmes should be subject to local management certification that they meet identified training needs.

The programmes chosen for purchase should be interesting, practical and job-related, and should cover a wide range of suitable subject areas.

Evaluating programmes can be a time-consuming job, and needs to be taken into account when planning a corporate learning centre. Selecting and stocking poor-quality programmes can adversely affect the centre's image and reputation. One bad experience and a learner may not come back again. It is important that only the best-quality courseware is stocked in the corporate learning centre.

Choosing courseware

Consider the possibility of obtaining inspection copies or sample material from suppliers for evaluation before purchase. Most suppliers will send you a demo disc for preview on request. This will help you judge how good and interactive the courseware is. Select a few staff with expertise in the particular subject area to examine the courseware, and ask their views about quality, standard and relevance. The same approach should be adopted for Internet-based e-learning programmes. Sample modules may be available for testing on the Internet. You could also visit suppliers and inspect the material on their premises. Many suppliers have viewing facilities on their premises. Another approach is to visit an organization which is already using a specific package, and seek feedback from them about the courseware's quality. Always weigh up the evaluation time against the cost and perceived importance of a programme.

Bespoke courseware

An important consideration is whether to lease or buy programmes off the shelf, or make them yourself. Because of the huge cost involved in creating in-house bespoke packages, this option is only feasible for large companies where a cost-benefit analysis shows that such an approach is justified by the savings achieved compared to using conventional training or purchasing commercial off-the-shelf packages. In other words, it can be justified if the capital cost involved can be spread over sufficient users. However, in the last few years the range and quality of commercial packages available for purchase off the shelf has improved enormously, so there is less need to develop bespoke courseware. Sometimes commercial packages can be customized to meet the specific needs of users at little extra cost.

Quality of courseware

Studies have also shown, unsurprisingly, that learners like well-designed courseware, but reject poor courseware. The quality of courseware will be measured according to various criteria, including:

- learner expectations
- how old the ideas or the presentation of the material appear to be
- online mentoring and tutorial support
- the relevance of the material to the learner's organization
- the length or complexity of the material
- its interactiveness and facility for collaborative learning
- how graphical and attractive the material is.

Learners tend to like or dislike various materials according to their different learning styles.

What makes a good package?

A good open learning package will enable a learner to work through the material alone, and to learn quickly and effectively. It must anticipate and deal satisfactorily with the types of problems and questions the average open learner will experience without the benefit of a face-to-face tutor. In evaluating open learning packages, consider the following points:

- What level is it aimed at – beginners or advanced?
- What format best suits your purpose – text, audio, video, CD-ROM/DVD or e-learning?
- Is it supported by user-friendly workbooks, if appropriate?
- Is it good value for money?
- Has it clear objectives, a modular structure and progress tests? Is it flexible? Can learners with different abilities and preferences take optional paths?
- Will it motivate the learner and sustain interest? Is it easy to understand and user-friendly? Does it use graphics to good effect?
- Does it meet a particular training need? Is it in harmony with the company's overall training and development strategy?
- Does it do the job of an existing 'live' programme, and thus free trainers for more demanding work?

Winning acceptability for open learning

How will employees react to the notion of a corporate learning centre, with its emphasis on self-learning, self-reliance and use of information technology? Will it become a hive of learning, or a white elephant – an under-utilized resource? Some companies have adopted corporate learning centres not on cost grounds, nor to meet training and development needs, and with little or no thought of how the centre should be supported or maintained. Where this is the case and senior management commitment dries up, the centre will just gradually die.

The mission, vision and purpose of the learning centre must be studied and linked with the overall training and development strategy, corporate objectives and business needs of the company. The practical implications should be examined, in particular how it will be integrated and used as part of an overall training plan. A senior manager of the company with a particular vision and interest in learning should be given the task of ensuring that the centre succeeds in the company's mission of providing lifelong learning opportunities that will benefit both the company and its employees. Similarly, in a multi-site situation it is important to make a local manager responsible for the success of the centre.

Many organizations have found that because clerical, administrative and professional staff are usually computer-literate, they take to computer-based training with great ease. After some initial guidance and tutor-based support, they become very self-sufficient open learners after a short time, and need only the minimum of tutor intervention. Manual workers often require more help because of their lack of a conceptual framework and familiarity with information technology and personal computers, particularly the Internet. Some may fear computers. Help should be provided by the corporate learning centre co-ordinator, who can gradually bring them to an appreciation of computers and the Internet with encouragement and sensitivity. Online mentoring and a helpdesk may be a feature of e-learning programmes.

There are now very good video-based computer appreciation courses which can be used to ease the process of induction and build up the learners' basic knowledge, confidence and frame of reference in computers. From these video courses, learners could graduate to a CD-ROM course on keyboarding skills.

Tapping personal development needs

To attract customers to the corporate learning centre, programmes of a social, recreational and personal development nature should also be stocked. The co-ordinator can then draw customers' attention to the wide range of other courses available. Personal development courses are often popular: for example, psychology courses dealing with interpersonal relations, self-esteem, assertiveness and confidence. Most of these courses are on audio and video tapes and CDs. This format is ideal for the person seeking to study in their own time. Some use personal stereos for listening to the audio tapes or CDs on their car stereos, while others listen to them as they commute to and from work.

The needs of part-time students should also be catered for. This is a growing area, with many employees studying on a part-time basis for certificate, diploma, degree and post-degree level with universities and professional institutes. There are a growing number of open learning programmes available to meet their specific needs, especially Internet-based e-learning programmes, and these should be accessible in the corporate learning centre. Many companies operate an educational support scheme to help these students to finance their studies.

Encouraging employees

The usage of the corporate learning centre should be monitored, which could include checking the number of loans to learners, including text, audio and video programmes for self-study at home. The aim should be to attract as wide a section of employees as possible, including operatives, clerical, accounting, administrative, supervisory, management, engineering and technical categories. Occasional fall-off in usage of the centre might be counteracted by an aggressive advertising and marketing drive, as appropriate. Employees who never use the centre or seldom use the centre should be especially targeted.

Encouraging managers

Sometimes managers may be resistant to using the corporate learning centre. They may lack keyboarding skills, as well as being unfamiliar with the basic equipment and peripherals. They don't want to look foolish in front of their computer-literate younger colleagues. Managers should be encouraged sign up for basic keyboarding, Internet and computer familiarization courses. Some banks have put their managers through the ECDL programme. New employees straight in from college are likely to be computer-literate and will have no hesitation in using the resources of the centre, which may be a source of embarrassment to managers.

Managers are often under a lot of work pressure. They may feel that time spent away from their desks in a corporate learning centre would not be looked on favourably by their peers and superiors: 'If he has time for open learning, maybe he's underemployed.' This attitude is regrettable. Managers more than anyone else should be seen to be updating their skills and keeping abreast of new thinking in business and management. Senior managers should encourage middle managers and supervisors to include corporate learning centre courses as part of their training and development, as well as undertaking such courses themselves.

Managers should set an example for their staff that lifelong learning is important, both for individuals and for the company, and is recognized as such. They should be the driving force in creating and sustaining a learning culture in the organization. It is a contradiction that senior managers authorize a huge financial investment in corporate learning centres, and then subsequently fail to support them in any visible fashion, either by allowing their staff time off to use the centre or by using it themselves.

Accessibility

The corporate learning centre should be accessible to all employees, and open at least during normal working hours. Ideally, it should open from 9.00 a.m. to 9.00 p.m. every day, although this may not be possible because of the cost of staffing. Outside these times, or normal working hours, the centre could be accessed by a special electronic magnetic card. This swipecard could be numerically controlled and issued to staff on request who want to use the centre after normal working hours.

'Smart' cards are available that will update the centre's learning management system. This will give the co-ordinator information on who used the centre, which course they undertook, the duration of the course, and so on. This facility will be particularly useful for shiftworkers, who need to plan their open learning around their working hours. With proper organization and planning, the centre may provide a 24-hour, round-the-clock service.

Sharing facilities

The capacity of the corporate learning centre can also be shared with other locations. In large regional-based organizations, open learning allows employees to obtain training in isolated locations where, because of inadequate demand, traditional training courses would be uneconomic to run. Computer networks, such as the Internet and intranet, mean that there is now no limit to the range of training courses that can be made available irrespective of the location. All you need is a PC and the right telecommunications infrastructure in place. These days, most employees have access to a computer in their workplace. Each PC is a potential mini-corporate learning centre in its own right, and can be linked to PCs in the main centre. Although Internet-based e-learning programmes and knowledge management systems facilitate this process, in practice it is often very difficult to ensure the right amount of quiet, uninterrupted time in the workplace.

Managers' role

Line managers can demonstrate their commitment to open learning and their interest in their staff by asking them for their views on corporate learning centre courses, and where they hope to apply the knowledge. They should also be encouraged to discuss the courses with their colleagues. Word-of-mouth recommendation may introduce new customers to the centre. Corporate learning centre courses, including Internet-based e-learning programmes, may be used as an introductory or refresher process for both knowledge and skills areas.

Managers should integrate corporate learning centre courses into the work routine by allowing staff to attend courses. Staff should be briefed before they go on courses, and debriefed when they return. In particular, they should be asked how they are going to apply the knowledge and skills learned. This displays an ongoing interest on the manager's part in the development of their staff. Managers should ensure that open learning is linked to better on-the-job performance, career progression and development. It should become standard practice at internal promotion interviews to ask candidates about the open learning programmes they have undertaken, and their application to on-the-job situations.

Pedagogy is a learning philosophy that assumes that the learner has a dependent personality. On the other hand, in andragogy the learner is assumed to be seeking increasing self-direction. The andragogic approach is more suitable in a work context. However, it should not be assumed that learners will voluntarily want to engage in corporate learning centre courses. They must have a job-specific reason for undertaking such programmes, and the organizational climate must be supportive. Managers are an important catalyst in this process.

Use it or lose it

Unless learners revise or apply knowledge or skills shortly after acquisition, they will lose them. To retain a skill, it must also be applied frequently. The corporate learning centre, close to the workplace, is a great way to refresh existing knowledge and keep abreast of new developments. It may be used to acquire knowledge and skill on a particular topic before attending a traditional 'live' course. Because learners have built up a conceptual framework of the material, they will find it easier to learn, while trainers can concentrate on the more difficult aspects of the course.

Open learning and the bottom line

The provision of a corporate learning centre is a practical demonstration of the organization's commitment to staff training and development, and visible evidence of learner empowerment. In practice, the concept of learner empowerment through open learning will be constrained by commercial and organizational factors, including the need to meet specified training objectives in line with corporate goals, and the need to translate them into relevant improvements in work practices and visible cost savings.

Hard-nosed managers with their eye on the bottom line often require tangible benefits in return for any investment in training. In times of recession, budgetary constraints will be a real problem as cutbacks bite into the training budget. Open learning must be shown to make a positive contribution through the quality of its courses and the transferability of the skills learnt to practical work situations. Line managers should be involved in the selection of suitable courseware and Internet-based e-learning programmes to meet the identified business and training needs in their areas of responsibility.

Learning management systems

Good learning management systems are available commercially for managing the administrative requirements of a corporate learning centre. Prickett (2002) reports that setting up an LMS can cost up to £40 000. These carry out all the recording necessary (such as time, type and description of course, and booth allocated) in booking learners into courses, tracking e-learning programmes, keeping tabs on learners' progress and recording loan-outs and returns of books, audio, CD and video packages. They should facilitate the production of personal development plans and collaborative learning. They should adhere to standards so that e-learning programmes and courseware are compatible. Ideally, they should support blended learning. In addition, they should be capable of integration with existing human resources systems and 'live' courses. They also provide comprehensive management information for individual training records and usage level of the courses. This information may be used to compare actual usage with standards, number of completions, popularity and job-relevancy of programmes, and the numbers and types of employee who are using the corporate learning centres. If the company has many centres in its organization, then comparative statistics may be compiled to see which courses and centres are the most successful, and why.

Carefully collated information will show which medium is the most popular – text, audio, CD, video, CD-ROM/DVD or Internet-based e-learning programmes. More importantly, it will highlight who is *not* using the centre. This information will help to focus marketing drives on the segments of the employee population who are not using the centre, or using it only infrequently, and will enable you to focus marketing drives on those segments of employees. Programmes not being used should be weeded out and discarded. Job-relevant courses or popular subject areas should be purchased or subscribed to. It is important that the corporate learning centres do not deteriorate into museums. The courses stocked or subscribed to should be current, job-relevant, in tune with the organizational culture, and frequently used.

Organizations with corporate learning centres

Corporate learning centres are now a well-established means for the delivery of training in progressive organizations in the UK and Ireland. In the UK, Lucas, British Steel, British Telecom and Norwich Union are some of the many who have established corporate learning centres. The majority of users tend to be large private- or public-sector organizations. In Ireland, corporate learning centres can be found in companies such as Aer Lingus, Guinness, FAS – The Irish Training Authority, Bank of Ireland, AIB Bank and Ulster Bank.

In May 2002, NETg announced a three-year strategic partnership with British Airways to supply e-learning services, including 500 courses. More than 50 000 British Airways employees, from pilots to baggage handlers, now have access to NETg's courses delivered predominantly on the company intranet and via its 30 corporate learning centres. For staff who do not have access to the intranet or corporate learning centres, CD-ROMs are made available. Courses include information technology, negotiation, coaching, project management and leadership skills. The e-learning courses will be used alongside existing classroom-based training.

Staff in IKEA Edinburgh, a furniture retailer, can access NETg e-learning programmes via a PC in the corporate learning centre, or can train at home on CD-ROMs. Managerial and supervisory staff are learning *Excel* and *PowerPoint*, while shopfloor staff are acquiring basic IT skills. Certification is available through the ECDL.

Computer Weekly (3 May 2001) reports that Derbyshire County Council has opened its seventh Learndirect centre in Glossop. Learndirect is the operational wing of UFI. The Learndirect centre courses are designed for people over 16 years of age who need to develop important workplace skills to equip them for the job market. Courses cover numeracy and literacy, business and management, Internet and computer skills. Each centre has ten networked Pentium III PCs running *Windows 2000* and packages such as desktop publishing.

Sloman (2001) reports how Motorola has set up learning centres at eight locations across the EMEA region (Europe, Middle East and Africa). A typical learning centre has networked PCs with an administrator available to offer support. Other learning resources available at these centres include books, videos, tapes, periodicals and language courses. E-learning is an important element in the learning mix.

Summary

To make the most out of your corporate learning centre you must:

- Identify training needs.
- Draw up a relevant syllabus to meet those needs.
- Evaluate open learning centre courses.
- Ensure that only the most job-relevant and best-quality courseware is selected and stocked, and that only the best e-learning programmes are subscribed to.

- Secure certification of some of your courses by linking up with outside colleges or through established e-learning programmes.
- Cater for the personal development needs of staff.
- Ensure employees' easy access to the centre during and after normal working hours.
- Make the most of your learning management system.
- Encourage your managers to actively support the learning centre.

4 Establishing costs and measuring benefits

Introduction

The costs of a corporate learning centre may be considered under two headings – *capital expenditure* and *revenue expenditure*. Capital expenditure is the cost of setting up and equipping the centre, while revenue expenditure is the cost of running the centre. You will need two budgets to control costs:

- a capital expenditure budget for equipment and premises
- a revenue or operating cost budget for software, overheads and running expenses.

In the following sections, we will consider these costs in some detail. It is useful to know the relative costs of the various media used in open learning, and to be aware of some of the success stories of the application of open learning in organizations.

Capital expenditure

Capital expenditure is the cost of setting up and equipping the centre. It involves premises, furniture and fittings, booths for learners, computer hardware and other equipment costs such as printers, television sets, CD-ROM/DVD players, audio cassette players, CD players and video players. There will also be a cost involved in fitting out the premises, including telecommunications networks, special electrical wiring, painting, carpets, plants and pictures. To become operational, the capital expenditure required may be anything from £25 000 to £125 000 depending on the number of booths, equipment and size of the accommodation. There will also be continuing costs of updating equipment and setting up other centres, if necessary.

Revenue expenditure

Revenue expenditure will include the co-ordinator's salary, light and heat, depreciation of equipment, maintenance and repair of premises and equipment, rent and rates, telephone charges, postage, stationery, cleaning, software costs and subscriptions for e-learning programmes. Revenue expenditure or running costs each year, assuming a full-time co-ordinator, may be around £75 000 per annum in an average centre. The size of this budget will be strongly influenced by the number, variety and quality of courseware provided.

Budget

A capital expenditure budget for equipment and a revenue expenditure budget for software, subscriptions for e-learning programmes and the operating costs of running the centre must be drawn up each year by the co-ordinator, who will agree it with the Training and Development manager. The management information system should provide monthly reports on budgets and actual amounts spent. These should be examined each month to ensure that costs are on target, and any overexpenditure investigated and accounted for.

Marketing costs

Marketing costs will be an important element in the corporate learning centres budget. There will be a one-off marketing cost when launching the corporate learning centre. Ongoing costs will include advertising in the form of the users' course guide, managers' course guide, brochures, posters, e-mail, and the cost of the quarterly newsletter. A competent co-ordinator may be able to conduct the marketing and thus keep costs down, but some outside printing costs may be inevitable, such as the course guides.

Videotapes

Training videos cost as little as £120 or as much as £3000. High price does not always guarantee high quality. They include workbooks and trainers' and participants' guides. Some are designed as training packages and can be run as 'live' workshops or worked through individually by learners. With the passage of time, fashions and best-practice standards change, so some videotapes should be replaced every few years.

Audiotapes/Compact Discs

A single audio tape may cost as little as £12 or less. Training packages consisting of six or more audiotapes complete with workbooks may cost considerably more, but still offer good value for money. A budget of a few thousand pounds will stock the corporate learning centre with a good selection of audio or CD programmes. But beware! Although there are many excellent audiotapes and CDs on the market, there are also many poor-quality programmes, so make sure you evaluate them before purchase.

Text-based courses

Books may cost as little as £10 each. Text-based courses consisting of trainers' and participants' guides cost considerably more, perhaps up to £200 per course. Don't be blinded by the hype about multimedia or technology-based training. Text-based resources remain a highly cost-effective development tool. Many learners still prefer working with books, and their needs should be catered for. Again, a budget of a few thousand pounds could stock up the corporate learning centre with a variety of good-quality course material.

Multimedia

Generic multimedia packages, including CD-ROM and DVD, start at about £1200, and can cost up to £3000 or more. You have to judge this cost in relation to the number of trainees that will use the programme, and the savings involved compared to traditional training. For bespoke e-learning programmes, costs will be in excess of £100 000. Wilson (2001) says that the cost of development for Web-based courseware is much higher than conventional classroom training. While costs vary, an estimate of £15 000-plus per hour of content is not uncommon. Obviously, the greater the number of employees involved in the programme, the less the training cost per trainee. They only become economical when large numbers have to be trained in a specific area. The main cost of multimedia lies in design and production.

In traditional training, the costs lie in travel, accommodation, disruption of work, overtime, trainer/learner time, stationery, and capital depreciation. For bespoke multimedia packages, the breakeven point is probably between 100 and 200 learners. With off-the-self courseware, it can be as little a 10 learners. Above these figures, significant savings are achieved. Budget £25 000 or more for generic multimedia, and £100 000 or more for bespoke programmes.

Authoring systems

Authoring tools enable trainers to integrate various media to create professional, engaging and interactive training content. Trainers take considerable time to become proficient in them. For example, Kattackal (1994) reports that a trainer typically takes 100 to 150 hours to produce each delivered hour of CBT, and six to nine months to develop a moderately complex multimedia course. Costs of authoring software ranges from a few hundred to a few thousand dollars. If the trainer uses video extensively, costs could reach $187 000 to $312 500, or about $12 500 to $25 000 per finished hour of training. Therefore, it is only the bigger companies which could afford to do their own courseware design, as the cost for even modest programmes is likely to run into thousands.

Harris (2002) reports that many organizations are attempting to reduce their training costs by developing e-learning materials in-house. He advises that authoring tool standards differ. If your organization is currently using a learning management system you need to ensure that it is compatible with the system considered. Consult your IT department for advice. There is always the possibility of subcontracting the work to an outside software house. Sloman (2001) reports that Clifford Chance, a London-based law firm, decided to construct its authoring facility in conjunction with a software specialist who would assist with customization and implementation. In any event, the expense of designing your own courseware can only be justified on a cost-benefit basis where large numbers of employees will use it and thus the cost per trainee will become economical.

Authoring your own programmes using existing off-the-shelf video or other materials likely to contravene the original producer's copyright, and may prove a legal minefield.

Profitability

Like any other business undertaking, corporate learning centres should be run on a commercial basis as profit centres. To make them cost-transparent and commercially viable, there should be a charge out for internal departments, and the centre should also be marketed externally. There are many different ways of changing that could be used. Some companies may see the corporate learning centre as a cost centre, and thus be satisfied with a recovery of costs. The centre might be charged to the user departments on bases such as number of employees or take-up of courses.

Other companies might like to treat the corporate learning centre on a more commercial basis and charge market rates for its services. Initially, they could be opened to staff family members on a fee-paying basis, and eventually opened up commercially to employees of other organisations. Off-the-shelf materials are sold for use within the purchasing organization only. Organizations wishing to open their centre to other organizations or individuals should check the copyright situation with the producers of the material they have purchased, to avoid risking litigation.

Cost savings

One of the key motivations behind the introduction of corporate learning centres is cost savings. Studies suggest that open learning is more cost-effective than traditional training. It saves trainer time and learner time off the job. As a learning medium, it is also more effective in some instances than other forms of training. Retention rates are higher, and learning is integrated into the job more quickly and better when it occurs near the workplace rather than 'away on a course'. However, line managers must be convinced by concrete evidence that corporate learning centres are cost-effective and do in fact meet real business and training needs. There is always the danger that they will appeal only to a minority of users and contribute little to organizational objectives.

The financial benefits of training are difficult to quantify. Nevertheless, it is important to quantify the savings and benefits of a corporate learning centre. In fact, the costs are relatively easy to establish. For example, e-learning programmes may be charged on a pay-as-you-view basis. Alternatively, an annual licence fee may be paid. The learning management system will contain information on the number of learners, courses taken, completion rates, duration of courses, popularity of courses, media used and so on. From the corporate learning centre budgets and this information, it will be possible to work out the cost per trainee hour. Comparisons can then be made with 'live' training conducted within the company or outside, and can be used to prove the cost-effectiveness of learning centre courses – the reduced cost of training. The financial savings in these and other costs saved can equally be easily quantified:

- travelling
- overnight accommodation

- reduced overtime
- less absence from the workplace.

Other benefits may be more difficult to quantify, but should nevertheless be considered, such as:

- improvements in productivity
- increased job satisfaction and morale
- improved quality
- better customer service
- increased confidence of employees
- improved career prospects.

Measuring the benefits

In general, the training provided by the corporate learning centre should be seen as a long-term investment and vote of confidence in people, rather than as a cost. Although not reflected directly on the balance sheet of a company, it is in fact an investment in intellectual capital, and will enhance the company's ability to make profits. It is more valuable than brands, which are often capitalized on the balance sheet. This enhancement in intellectual capital has a real value, and may be quantified in management accounts just as some companies do for brands in the financial accounts. The investment in intellectual capital will reap many benefits in the future, including a knowledge-based added value which will prove to be the key competitive advantage in an information-driven society. It is the creativity, skill and knowledge of the workforce which will make the profits for the company and determine its success or failure.

Surveys of open learners and their managers should be taken from time to time to establish satisfaction levels with the corporate learning centre. In particular, the co-ordinator should obtain feedback on actual applications and benefits of corporate learning courses to on-the-job situations. Managers might be asked to quantify any financial savings achieved. On the basis of this feedback, improvements should be made, and the centre's philosophy should be to make continuous improvements in the range of courses and services on offer. It is also necessary to keep in touch with what is happening in the outside world. This can be maintained through contact with other companies using corporate learning centres, colleges involved in distance learning, suppliers, e-learning providers, user associations and courseware exhibitions. The Internet may assist in this process.

From the learning management system, statistics may be compiled of the numbers using the centre, learning in progress, completions, the types of courses used, popularity, their frequency and duration. A top ten list of the most popular courses can be identified, and more importantly, the least popular can be marked out for possible removal. This information can be classified by department, division, grade of employee, age, gender and so on. It will be invaluable in discovering the areas of the company which are benefiting from corporate learning centre courses.

Companies claiming benefits and savings

Open learning may be a cost-effective way of bringing training to those who need it most. Chute et al. (1990) highlight an AT&T study which showed that the actual cost of technology-based training is lower than traditional training.

Many organizations have found the investment in corporate learning centres to be cost-effective although the cost of developing computer courseware or e-learning programmes is high and can only be justified if it can be spread over a large number of trainees. Managers argue that the initial costs of installing new equipment and buying or producing course materials are offset by less need for trainers, and other savings. This is because staff learn either in their own time or at work, instead of off-site in the company's training college or attending external training establishments.

Sloman (2001) reports that in 1998 the Post Office set up six pilot learning centres in different parts of the UK. These were aimed at front-line staff, were free, and could be accessed during the three shifts. Computer packages were available, together with other training resources. Someone was available to assist learners when required. These centres were deemed to be successful where they were actively marketed. Since then, the Post Office has been exploiting the opportunities for e-learning on its intranet.

Dillich (2000) reports that companies realize that enhancing employee skills is key to creating a sustainable competitive advantage. Also, companies which offer ongoing education and training enjoy a high rate of employee retention and the benefits of a better-skilled workforce. In fact, young professionals are now demanding that employers provide them with ongoing training and development opportunities.

Martin (2001) reports in a recent ASTD study, firms with an average investment of $1595 per employee in training experience 24 per cent higher gross margins and 218 per cent higher sales revenue per employee.

Galagan (2001) reports that there have been substantial savings from e-learning programmes at Cisco. Assembly line workers have access to e-learning on the factory floor. Result – savings of $1 million per quarter, and employees acquire skills faster.

Lamb (2002) reports that IBM has saved $200 million per year on the cost of training its 95 000 employees worldwide by switching to e-learning. Similarly, Dow Chemicals has saved $100 million by providing 80 per cent of its health and safety training over the Internet. An added bonus is the ability to manage and assess the progress of trainees. Savings accrue from lower travel costs, smaller hotel charges, less time off work and the more effective learning styles facilitated by Web-based courses. IBM expect to scale back training centres and instructor-led training.

Cutbacks in training budgets

In every annual report, organizations refer to the key role people play in the success of their business. However, the same organizations are often reluctant and sceptical about investing in those people through training and development programmes. In fact, in times of recession one of the first budgets to be reduced, or indeed eliminated, is the Training and Development budget. This is because it is so easy to cut, and seemingly painless. Its cost-reduction consequences are felt immediately, but the strategic implications of a reduction in training may not be felt for some years.

Many commentators see the Germans' vocational training system as a critical component of their economic success. Similar claims have been made for the Japanese approach to training. On the other hand, in Britain and Ireland our attitude to training leaves a lot to be desired, as reflected in our much smaller investment in training. Training must be taken seriously if we are to make a successful transition to the knowledge-based society and compete successfully with the Germans and Japanese.

Summary

The costs involved in establishing and running a corporate learning centre can be classified under the two headings of *capital expenditure* and *revenue expenditure*. Capital expenditure is the cost of setting up the centre and acquiring the premises and equipment. Revenue expenditure is the cost of operating the centre. Revenue expenditure is the operating cost, and will include marketing costs.

The different costs associated with the various media used in open learning were highlighted. In addition, the costs and benefits of running a corporate learning centre were identified, and examples given of some companies who claim significant savings and benefits as a result of their use.

5 How to resolve resistance to change

Introduction

In the modern world, organizations are faced with rapid change – political, legal, economic, social, technological and competitive. Organizations can decide to ignore change and risk extinction, or actively decide to manage change. A proactive approach to training and development is needed to maintain a competitive advantage. New technology has provided new delivery systems such as e-learning for education and training. It would be very short-sighted to ignore these developments. The corporate learning centre approach, incorporating Internet-based e-learning programmes, is an essential ingredient of any progressive training and development strategy, a useful addition to the range of training resources, and a positive response to managing change.

There are many reasons why employees might resist the idea of learning through corporate learning centres, including natural resistance to change, fear of the unknown, technophobia, work pressures, an unsupportive organizational climate, lack of learning skills, poor motivation, unenthusiastic management, special needs and domestic or other commitments. This chapter will explore these resistances in some more detail, and suggest ways in which they might be overcome.

Force field analysis

A useful model for understanding change is called *force field analysis*. This technique can be used to anticipate, analyse and understand the various forces acting for and against change. If you anticipate and plan for change, then you can be prepared for the likely arguments against it. In this model, change is seen as the outcome of some forces which tend to bring change about, and other forces which tend to resist change. Change is facilitated through the reduction or elimination of the resisting forces, and through strengthening the driving forces.

The driving forces of change

The driving forces might include:

- competition, meaning that the company must make its training more cost-effective
- the need for employee training in information technology skills
- the need to decentralize training and make it available to all employees
- employee desire for empowerment
- the support of boardroom management.

The restraining forces of change

The restraining forces might include:

- a company culture that is bureaucratic and resists any change
- managers sceptical about open learning
- trainers seeing open learning as a threat to their jobs
- high initial capital investment, with the return seen as uncertain
- no existing tradition or experience in the company in computer-based training.

Figure 5.1 shows the result of a force field analysis on the situation. A number of restraining forces have been identified, and the relative importance of each shown in relation to the size of the arrowed line (longer lines imply more importance). In this example, the effective implementation of a corporate learning centre will be restrained by the culture of the company and the scepticism of managers about open learning, the resistance of trainers who see open learning as a threat to their jobs, the high capital investment required, and the uncertain return. Similarly, a number of driving forces have also been identified, including the need to maintain competitiveness, pressure from boardroom management, and the desire to decentralize training.

The decisionmaker can now use the analysis to evaluate how the

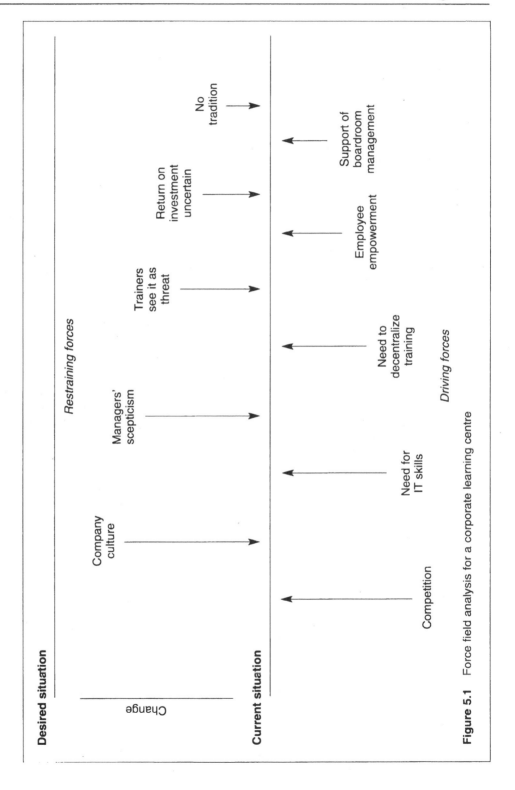

Figure 5.1   Force field analysis for a corporate learning centre

restraining factors might be removed or reduced, and how to reinforce the driving forces.

Wrong organizational climate

Indicator	*Reason*
Lack of top management support.	Senior managers see training as a cost, rather than an investment. They prefer to buy in staff with the necessary expertise.
Initial top management support, which then wanes.	Senior managers initially support open learning and the creation of a centre not because they believe in the centre, but because they perceive it as cheaper than traditional training.
Managers pay lip service to the centre but then fail to support it themselves, fail to encourage staff to use the centre, and even make it difficult for staff to put aside time for learning.	The managers have not been convinced of the real benefit to their team of open learning. This may be because of a perceived lack of support among senior managers.
Managers and supervisors actively discourage staff from using the centre.	Lack of direction from senior managers. Fear that well-trained staff may either be a threat to them, or that these staff will move to other companies or be poached.
Managers and supervisors are short term-oriented. Their immediate priorities relate to getting the work done in their own sections.	They lack the vision that the company will have skills needs and management succession needs in the future, and that training and development is vital to the strategic success of the company.
Managers feel that training raises the expectations of staff which cannot be met.	The current de-layering policy of many organizations means that there will be fewer opportunities for promotion in the future, so overqualified staff may feel frustrated and disillusioned.

Resolving these problems isn't easy, but it is essential to win support from senior and middle management and to develop the right climate for learning within the organization before you start if the centre is to have any hope of succeeding. The following techniques will help to resolve the problems.

Top management briefing

First, it is important to sell the concept fully to senior managers. They need to understand:

- what the centre can and cannot offer to employees and the organization
- what the strengths and weaknesses of computer-based training are
- what the set-up costs and the running costs will be
- how the centre will fit into the context of training within the organization
- what impact it will have on the hours worked by employees using the centre
- what the future strategy of the centre is likely to be.

At this stage, you should encourage all and any questions and establish support. If you can secure commitment from the senior managers to concrete action, such as their agreement to brief managers and staff to visit the centre themselves, then so much the better.

Their initial commitment is only the first step. You'll need to keep them regularly briefed on your progress. The statistics you gather on usage of the centre, along with any feedback and research you can generate from users and their managers, will all provide you with evidence of the growing impact and success of the centre.

Middle managers

Briefing the middle managers might be done in an informal way, perhaps by chatting with them individually in the canteen or buttonholing individuals for a five-minute chat when they arrive at work. It is just as important as the top management briefing.

Once again, you need to ensure that the managers understand what the centre can offer them and their staff. They will also need to understand and give their commitment to supporting their staff, by allowing them time to learn, encouraging them to use the centre, and taking an active interest in their development. This would include follow-up action to ensure that staff regularly attend relevant corporate learning centre courses to meet identified training needs and corporate strategic requirements. You may choose to remind managers that they have line responsibility for the training and development of their staff. Potential learners look to their managers as role models, so encourage the managers themselves to use and enthuse about the centre.

Participation councils

Many large companies use participation councils as a channel of communication with employees. Council members are often the informal leaders of work groups, and thus a great channel through which to promulgate the benefits of open learning generally in the company. Emphasize that open learning can improve employees' job skills, personal development and career prospects within the company. The important benefit of accessibility for all employees regardless of age, status or previous education should also be stressed.

Trainers' resistance to change

Resistance to change will come from potential customers, but it is also likely to come from training staff themselves. They may see the introduction of corporate learning centres to the company as a threat to their jobs. It is true that some forms of training may be undertaken more cost-effectively through open learning. However, this should be seen as complementary to live training, rather than a substitute for it. It will free trainers to concentrate on the more difficult, demanding, practical and company-specific aspects, such as identifying training needs and evaluating training. It will also give them an opportunity to develop their mentoring and coaching roles. They can at last take on the role of facilitator, rather than instructor.

Much of the knowledge and theory aspects of training programmes may be delegated to the corporate learning centre. As part of group training programmes, course participants can be told to work through relevant corporate learning centre courseware before they come on the 'live' training course. The time span of such courses can thus be reduced, and trainers will have more time to concentrate on the more challenging and interactive aspects of training, such as projects, case studies, role-play, interpersonal relations skills and teamwork. This job enrichment will provide more job satisfaction for the trainer, and ultimately reduce the direct cost of 'live' training, which becomes more focused and relevant. In addition, preparation time and the cost of producing handouts and transparencies is saved.

The message must be understood by trainers – there is no threat to their jobs. The only difference will be that their jobs will become more interesting, as the routine aspects of training will be taken over by the corporate learning centre. Any reduction in the number of trainers should be through natural wastage and non-replacement. This will free the trainers to develop new skills, to concentrate on the more demanding and interesting aspects of training, and to develop their facilitating role.

Learners' resistance to change

There is a natural resistance to change in most people. They prefer to keep on doing what they're used to doing. In psychology, this is known as the *comfort zone*. Mature people, in particular, seem to prefer routine, and sometimes fear the inevitable arrival of the new information technology. This is unlike the younger generation, who have grown up with modern PCs and treat them as an ordinary, everyday gadget just like television or any other modern appliance.

Good communications, education, training and marketing should be part of the battle to change attitudes and overcome this resistance to the use of information technology, and open learning in particular. Open learning should be part of the approach to equip employees to cope with change.

Reluctant employees

Some staff lack the intrinsic motivation to undertake any sort of formal new learning experience. They are content with their lot, lack ambition, and thus don't see the need to undertake any open learning courses. They know how to do their existing job, so why bother with anything else? They don't seem to realize that there are now no guarantees of jobs for life, and that new skills must be developed on an ongoing basis if one is to survive in the modern workplace. In fact, the more skills you possess, the more marketable you will become – not only to your own employer, but to potential outside employers as well. These staff require special consideration, and need to be offered incentives to use the corporate learning centres. They are probably the ones who need training the most, but are the least likely to receive it. One way around this problem might be to give such staff monetary incentives to enrol in corporate learning centre courses. Certainly, managers and supervisors should particularly encourage these employees.

Fear

Another barrier is a psychological fear of any formalized new learning, including open learning and traditional training. Many fear any form of institutional learning. This could be a throwback to schooldays, with associations of failure, inferiority, punishment, teacher/authority figures, competition and classrooms. The prospect of 'making a fool of themselves' or appearing 'stupid' in front of peers in a traditional training situation can deter them from attending a course. One of the great advantages of open learning is that you can make your mistakes in private. No one need know about them, and nobody is breathing down your neck. Of course, learning from your mistakes is the best route to effective learning.

A middle-aged person who wants to learn new skills may feel inadequate, uncomfortable and threatened on a 'live' course with much younger people. However, with the right support, encouragement and a favourable environment, they often become the best, most committed and most highly motivated open learners. Learning is often wasted on the young, who do not savour the opportunity they are offered to enhance their education and training.

Corporate learning centres provide a non-threatening, supportive environment for learners, with none of the competition and stress associated with traditional training. Nevertheless, some learners fear the unstructured nature of open learning. It is important that the co-ordinator informs the learner of the difference between traditional training and open learning, and stresses the benefits of the latter. The co-ordinator should be supportive and facilitative rather than intrusive. The learner will appreciate the opportunity to experiment with new ideas and approaches without peer pressure or trainer interference.

Domestic commitments

For many adults, work is not their only responsibility. Their families also need consideration and demand attention. For personal success, harmony and happiness, individuals need to create balance in their lives. There is a time to work, and a time to play. Time for yourself and your family is important. Working parents may find difficulty in arranging childcare or crèche facilities to attend courses that require travel and overnight stays.

Corporate learning centre courses can be taken at a time which suits parents' working arrangements, domestic situations and lifestyle. Managers and supervisors should have regard to employee lifestyles, and try to accommodate their needs with individual training plans making use of the accessibility and flexibility of corporate learning centre courses. They should be generous in their approach to allowing such employees time off during the work day to attend such courses. It may even be a good idea to provide crèche facilities adjacent to the corporate learning centre for employees with children. This would certainly be visible support on the company's part.

Work pressures

Many employees have difficulty finding time to take part in corporate learning centre courses during the working day, and are too tired to do so during their free time. Tight staffing arrangements and work deadlines mean this may sometimes be a problem in functional departments, but it is particularly acute in operational areas.

Some flexibility in staffing arrangements is needed to facilitate staff in operational areas to take up corporate learning centre courses. In practice, large companies and public-sector organizations tend to be more flexible in this area than smaller firms. An allowance of two hours per week per employee for relevant corporate learning centre courses would not seem to be unreasonable. For important courses, a more generous block of time may be allocated, depending on the nature of the course and how relevant and urgent it is to the requirements of the job.

Learners with special needs

Although there have been vast improvements in access to buildings in recent years, it can still be very difficult for people with physical disabilities to attend traditional training courses in training and educational establishments. Making arrangements for special transport can add to the problems.

These problems are mostly overcome with corporate learning centre courses. At the design and planning stage of the centre, the necessary modifications should be considered to cater for the physically disabled. Subsequent alterations may prove to be very expensive. An organization which cares for the training needs of physically disabled employees is seen as caring and progressive, and will not hesitate to invest in their needs.

Conventional computer-based training programmes are not suitable for the deaf or blind or those who have poor literacy and numeracy skills. Specially designed computer-based technology is available to help the visually impaired and the deaf to learn. In addition, there are very good programmes designed to help people with poor literacy and numeracy skills.

Lack of study skills

Staff who have been away from formal learning situations for a long time may feel they lack the study skills, time management skills, willpower, concentration and mental discipline necessary to study an open learning programme. Many may not have any conventional educational qualifications or have undertaken any formal systematic study in the past.

A CD-ROM programme on study skills called 'Learning to Learn' is available, which staff can work through before they undertake an open learning centre course. There are also many very good texts on study and learning skills available, including some from the authors of 'Learning to Learn', published by CIMA of London. Corporate learning centres should stock them and encourage newcomers to use them.

Isolation

Learners may feel a sense of isolation when undertaking corporate learning centre courses, and miss the social interaction, teamwork, comradeship, contact and stimulation of 'live' training. In fact, our whole education system has taught us to be passive rather than self-directed, active learners. It takes some time to get used to the idea that we are responsible for our own learning, and it requires a radical change of attitude on our part. People must learn to learn themselves, and not wait around for other people to show them.

The 'drop in and help yourself to learning' philosophy of the corporate learning centre should help to overcome the attitude of dependence on others for learning. Tutorial support from the centre's co-ordinator may help to alleviate the problem. Schlechter (1990) found that small-group CBT was five times more cost-effective than individual CBT, and that learning effectiveness was increased. This supports the idea of collaborative learning, and suggests that the co-ordinator should encourage learners to learn in pairs, which would reduce isolation while improving performance. Learners might also be encouraged to set up 'self-help' groups using Internet chatrooms and e-mail. This will help to overcome the isolation problem. Support may also come from specialist experts in the organization, line managers and mentors.

Boredom

It is a well-established fact that the human attention span is between 20 and 40 minutes. Short breaks every half hour or so should be part of any learner's course in the corporate learning centre. Breaks maximize retention and learning, and provide time for reflection and consolidation of learning. Programmes selected for the centre should be relevant to the business needs of the company, modular in structure, and colourful, graphical and interactive, with plenty of feedback. This will help maintain concentration and interest, and reduce boredom.

The CD-ROM/DVD and e-learning courses now available use all the advantages of multimedia, with colour, sound, graphics and moving pictures. A picture speaks more than a thousand words. Colour enhances memory, while variety helps to maintain attention and concentration.

Many of these courses use the latest ideas from educational technology and are very interactive, and thus optimize the learning process and prevent boredom. E-learning, in particular, is designed for collaborative learning with online mentoring, e-mail and chatrooms.

Confidence

In practice, some people lack the confidence and self-esteem required to undertake any form of open learning course. They will have to be weaned gradually onto the open learning idea, and given a lot of support and guidance from the beginning.

Initially, to break them in, they may be encouraged to take audio- and video-based programmes. Eventually, many may develop the confidence to progress further and pursue some CD-ROM/DVD and e-learning courses. However, such people must be handled with a lot of patience, sensitivity and care. They should be made aware that learning a new subject, especially through a new medium, is not easy, but requires application, practice and persistence over time if one is to become successful, and that most people going back to learning after many years' absence have feelings of inadequacy.

Enabling learners to be effective

Research shows that adult learners require the following supports and basic skills if they want to learn effectively:

- They should be motivated – They should have a clear reason and purpose for learning. They like to be challenged just beyond their present level of ability. If challenged too much, they become stressed and demotivated and give up. If challenged too little, they become bored and switch off. The co-ordinator and mentors can assist by providing direction, challenge and purpose.

- They need clear objectives – Learners learn more effectively if they have an overview of the topic that they need to learn and clear objectives to aim for.

- They need to operate to a plan – Time schedules with interim goals and objectives should be a feature of the plan, with rewards for the achievement of objectives.

- They need feedback on progress during the learning process – This might include tests, questionnaires and checklists, which are an in-built feature of good computer-based training programmes.

- The learning must be relevant to their current or future needs.

- They should be able to learn at their own pace in a supportive environment, without stress and time pressures, which are barriers to learning – A learning environment with the right mood and atmosphere is important. Co-ordinators should create feelings of belonging, recognition and respect. Remember, the sweetest sound to a person is the sound of their own name. They like to be treated as equals, and should be given freedom to express their own views.

- They need to be able to integrate prior knowledge and work experience with the new learning – When they return to their jobs, they should be encouraged to apply the skills and knowledge learnt. The quicker they can do this, the more effective the transfer of learning.

- Ideally, they need to have developed 'learning how to learn' skills, such as confidence, time management, presentation, Mind Maps®, reading and memory skills.

- An adult's past experience may become an obstacle to new learning – They may have to unlearn negative attitudes towards learning, old ways of doing things, long-held prejudices and stereotypical thinking.

- It would be wrong to think that adult learners are a homogeneous group – They differ in terms of class, gender, culture, race, personality, learning style and life experience. The co-ordinator should also be aware of these factors when dealing with them.

Risks/threats to the centre

The main challenge of any open learning facility is that many staff do not use it because of pressing demands and deadlines during work time, and they are often expected to use it during their own time without sufficient incentives. In practice, how do you get staff in such circumstances to use the corporate learning centre? The answer is, of course, that you must provide them with the opportunity and time to use the centre, as well as the encouragement and example, otherwise there is always the danger that the centre will become nothing more than an expensive 'corporate toy', or in a worse scenario, a 'white elephant'. Even if open learning is used, evaluation is needed to assess its effectiveness in meeting business needs, and the extent to which the knowledge and skill are being transferred to the workplace.

Summary

Force field analysis is a useful model for helping managers understand and resolve resistance to change. The decisionmaker needs to use the analysis to evaluate how the restraining factors can be removed or reduced, and how the driving forces can be reinforced. Education, communication, participation and aggressive marketing are all ways to reduce or overcome resistance from employees to open learning. Managers and trainers may also be unenthusiastic about the introduction of corporate learning centres. Management's lack of support, commitment and encouragement should be acknowledged and overcome. The idea of open learning may be seen as a threat by trainers, so they must be sold the idea, to win their support.

6 Launching a corporate learning centre

Introduction

Preparation and planning is the key to success in launching a corporate learning centre. Failure to plan is planning to fail. The centre must be set up, fully equipped and furnished with good-quality courseware and ready to go. The syllabus or guide to courses will have been printed, and the initial marketing and advertising completed. The co-ordinator will have been appointed and trained in the requirements of the job. A good learning management system will have been installed and tested so that booking and student records can be kept. The chief executive or local celebrity will have been booked to make the launch, and the press invited to attend.

Benchmarking

Before finally committing yourself, you should visit a few companies which have successfully set up corporate learning centres. Find out at first hand what were the problems they encountered and how they overcome them. Ask them how they went about organizing the launch, who they invited and so on. This information will prove invaluable. Benchmark your learning centre against the best you saw, and plan to do even better. On an ongoing basis, develop partnerships and networks with centres in other organizations to learn from their experience.

Networking PCs

In a large, geographically dispersed organization, you may be considering opening several corporate learning centres. Using a local area network (LAN), PCs in the same building can be linked together. Similarly, PCs over a wider geographical area can be linked together using wide area networks (WANs). WANs are an obvious choice for companies with geographically dispersed regions or branch networks. Special telecommunications systems are needed to support the Internet and intranets, and the cost of this must be compared to standalone centres before a final decision is made. However, these networks have obvious advantages compared with standalone centres. With the latter, each centre will have to carry its own courseware. With networks, the same courseware can be shared, and should thus be more economical.

Location

Corporate learning centres should be strategically located where there are high concentrations of employees, and where they are easily accessible and highly visible. The best location is on the ground floor, near the reception area and main entrance to the building. This creates maximum visibility and accessibility, especially for the disabled, whose needs should be considered when designing the centre. Think about those employees who will be using the centre at night. It should be easy to find, and the approach to the centre should be well lit and signposted. A location near the main entrance to the building will also encourage a high level of 'passing trade'.

Reception area

The reception area is used for counselling, course appraisal, administration, course enquiries and storage of learning materials, and generally for meeting customers and visitors. Ideally, it should be designed to minimize disruption to other learners and to respect the privacy of learners. A quiet study atmosphere with minimum distraction is needed if learners are to concentrate and maintain self-discipline. A friendly and welcoming approach by the co-ordinator will create the right mood.

Logo and signposting

Put up a large, attractive sign on the door with the logo: 'Walk in and help yourself to knowledge.' The door of the corporate learning centre should always be kept open. This is part of the policy of removing barriers to learning. The logo should be instantly recognizable as signifying a corporate learning centre. The creation of brand awareness and loyalty is an important goal. The logo should become synonymous with the centre. A dedicated Website on the intranet will help to create brand-awareness.

Layout and equipment

You will need a dedicated room for the corporate learning centre. See Figure 6.1 for a suggested layout. Ideally, the room should be custom-built, but in reality this is often not the case and you must make do with the conversion of existing vacant office accommodation. The size of the room is determined by the number of booths needed for learners, the reception area, co-ordinator's desk and display and storage facilities. Each booth should be dedicated to a particular type of equipment and specific range of courseware. A laminated poster giving a general list of courses available may be displayed in a prominent place on the side of each booth. The individual workstations should provide comfort, seclusion and privacy for up to two learners, or indeed for one learner with tutor support. Chairs should be ergonomically designed to prevent backache and maximize comfort. Tables should be of the appropriate height, with plenty of surface space for working on.

The PCs in the booth should be linked up to the Internet and to a printer, so that learners can access e-learning programmes and print out their work if they wish. A colour printer might be considered for learners who want to print out the results of graphical packages such as *Harvard Graphics*, *Freelance Graphics* and *PowerPoint*. This facility has the added advantage of training learners in the use of printers.

Study Booths

The number, nature and layout of the study booths within the centre will depend on the following factors:

- number of customers expected to use the centre at any one time
- number of employees in the immediate catchment area
- shape and size of the room available
- furniture, equipment, media and courseware selected
- number of subjects catered for, and their likely popularity
- budget allocated for setting up and equipping the centre
- particular needs of departments or locations.

In general terms, each booth should be supplied with:

- electrical and other sockets for equipment
- individual lighting, if required

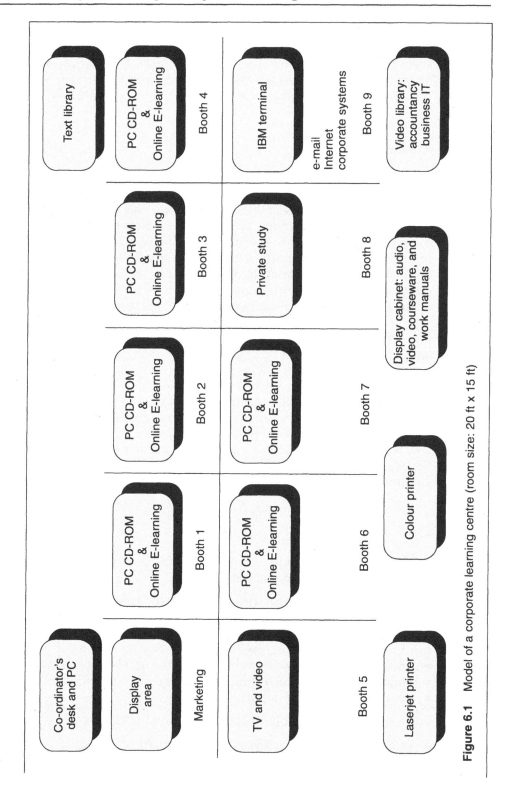

Figure 6.1   Model of a corporate learning centre (room size: 20 ft x 15 ft)

- adequate space for writing and coursework
- shelving to temporarily store books, manuals or other materials.

Figure 6.2 suggests how an eight-booth centre might be dedicated.

Large centres may also have a booth dedicated to the teaching of corporate systems, such as the personnel management information system, the management accounting and cost control system, and the marketing information system. These systems may be on the mainframe computer, with access via a computer terminal from the corporate learning centre. This booth may also provide tutorials on e-mail and the Internet.

Depending on the type of business, booths might also be dedicated to production, technical and engineering subjects. Health and safety is another area which is topical and for which courseware and e-learning programmes are available. The subjects will depend on the needs of your particular business.

There should be a high standard of furnishing so that the centre is attractive to work in, with sufficient equipment to accommodate the courseware.

Co-ordinator's desk

The basic requirements for the co-ordinator will be a PC and a telephone. The PC should include a good learning management system, and software programme with word-processing, desktop publishing, spreadsheet and graphical capabilities. These packages will be needed for marketing and advertising, such as producing brochures, posters and a newsletter. The co-ordinator will also need e-mail and Internet and intranet access. The e-mail is useful as a mentoring, marketing and communications tool with learners both inside and outside the organization.

Text library

One display cabinet should be used for books and text-based programmes. Subject classification will be helpful to learners, as well as your own coding system to keep track of titles. Some subjects can go out of date quickly – make sure you stock the latest editions.

Video library

Another display cabinet may be used for videos. These should also be kept in subject order and within subject by code order, and displayed at eye level, if possible.

Booth	Format	Subjects (Depend on company needs)	Notes
1 & 2	CD-ROM & Online E-learning	Keyboarding, word processing, spreadsheets, graphics, general IT skills	Large demand for IT skills requires two dedicated booths
3	CD-ROM & Online E-learning	Economics, management, marketing, financial accounting, costing, management accounting	Popular with staff studying formal qualifications
4	CD-ROM & Online E-learning	Management and personal development	
5	TV and video	Accounting, finance, marketing, management, languages, IT	
6	Audio	Management and personal development	
7	Books, magazines etc.	Private study, reading and research	
8	Terminal	Corporate systems, e-mail and networks	Tutorials on PMIS, MOCCS, e-mail etc.

Figure 6.2   Dedicated booths

Audio/CD library

This may be a separate display cabinet, or may be shared with the text or video library. Special storage units can be purchased for storing audiotapes and CDs. They should be kept by subject and within subject by code order.

General display cabinet

CD-ROM and DVD packages and their associated workbooks and documentation may be stored in a general display cabinet. Display cabinets should be attractive, and organized so that users can see the contents clearly and, if possible, at eye level. Depending on the size and variety of courses stocked, it might be a good idea to organize them by subject area or by media – for example, books, audio, video and computer courseware – and within the media classification by subject area. Each item should have a learning centre code number. However, whatever the classification system, it should be user-friendly. Courseware and indeed e-learning programmes start to become out of date as soon as they are made, and so need to be kept under constant review, both for physical condition and relevance.

General information stand

Provision should be made for a general information stand to display the corporate learning centre catalogue, users' guide to courses, health and welfare literature, college brochures offering part-time courses and new and popular open learning programmes. Corporate videos such as those on the annual report and accounts, strategic plan or safety could also be displayed. This is a type of sales promotion, and can generate interest and business from people who just 'pop in' out of curiosity to see what the corporate learning centre is all about. It is a focal and talking point, and gives the co-ordinator an opportunity to engage the client in conversation about courses on offer and to sell the centre.

The learning environment

A corporate learning centre must be a comfortable and pleasant place to work in. Further design considerations should include:

- adequate toilet facilities and drinking water facilities nearby
- heating, lighting and ventilation of a high standard, and with minimum noise disturbance

- lighting positioned in such a way that it does not shine directly onto the computer screen
- window blinds, if necessary, to prevent sunlight shining onto computer screens
- air conditioning
- VDUs fitted with anti-glare screens
- health and safety legislation.

State-of-the-art decor and equipment will look professional. The room should be soundproofed, carpeted and brightly painted, with bright, colourful pictures on the wall. Warm colours create the right ambience for learning. The pictures should have a relaxing, learning and educational theme. Suppliers' posters may be suitable, and these should be framed. Plants strategically situated around the room will add to the atmosphere of peace, learning and relaxation. Every effort should be made to make the environment conducive to learning, and non-threatening.

Soft Classical baroque music is reputed to enhance learning effectiveness and memory, and may be played in the background. It has a rhythm of one beat per second or 60 beats per minute. Users of corporate learning centres where this background music is played confirm that they find it enjoyable, relaxing and conducive to learning.

Technical support

Technical support may be provided within the organization or from outside. There are companies that will lease the hardware, supply the software and provide technical support all in one package. Others provide a complete e-learning solution with virtual learning centres. There is no doubt that problems will arise from time to time with hardware and software, and technical support must be available quickly to solve them.

The co-ordinator should be trained to diagnose and solve routine problems. A booklet on routine maintenance and troubleshooting should be compiled as a reference. Thus the co-ordinator should have good knowledge of PCs, associated equipment and operating systems. Technical support for software is often provided by the suppliers. However, problems associated with hardware should be left to the experts.

In practice, modern technology is becoming more reliable. Nevertheless, when there are problems it is essential that help is quickly at hand. Therefore, whoever gets the maintenance contract must be fast, efficient and reliable. There is nothing more frustrating from a user's point of view than having learning appointments cancelled because of malfunctioning hardware and software. From the co-ordinator's viewpoint, the loss of business may be difficult to make up.

Why establish a centre?

A corporate learning centre should meet real business and training needs. Market research should be carried out to establish what the likely demand for a centre would be. Research could take the form of face-to-face or telephone interviews using a questionnaire.

Piloting

Where there are a number of corporate learning centres to be set up in the organization, it might be a good idea to run a pilot centre initially to test out the concept. If it works, then the other centres could be opened up gradually. The advantage of this approach is that one can learn from mistakes made, and take corrective action in subsequent centres.

Pre-launch planning

If the market research is favourable, then after the centre has been set up, the official launch could be planned. Before the official launch, the organization should carry out a major communications and marketing drive to increase staff awareness of the purpose and concept of corporate learning centres, the advantages of open learning, the location of the centre, the type of media used, the duration of courses, and the range of courses stocked. Now is the opportunity to sell the benefits of the centre to:

- employees (and overcome their resistance)
- managers (and overcome their resistance)
- directors (and win their support)
- reinforce the organization's commitment to individual development, to learning, and the achievement of corporate objectives.
- reinforce the importance of the centre in the eyes of the employees, by chief executive and director-level participation and the involvement of external dignitaries (the local mayor if you wanted to use the centre to highlight the organization's importance to the local community, or other appropriate celebrities if you wanted to suggest that learning is 'OK').

A chart of the of the corporate learning centre project plan is shown in Figure 6.3.

Selling to managers

Talk to as many managers and staff as possible, and let them know about the forthcoming launch of the corporate learning centre, and the facilities that will be available.

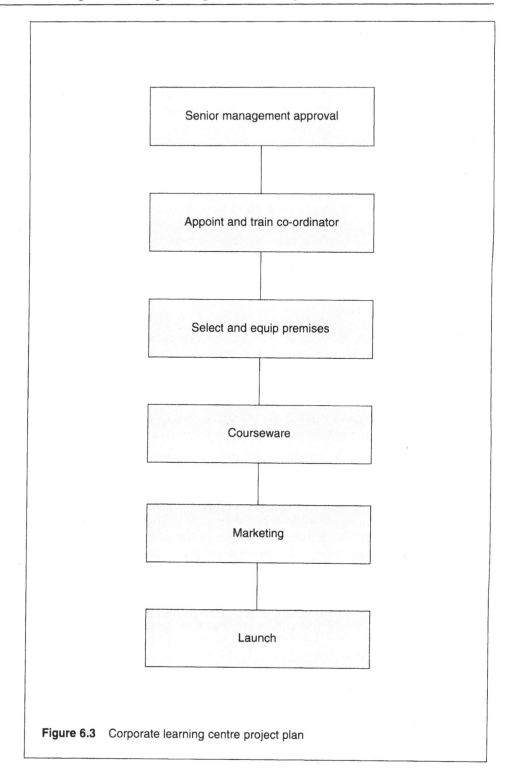

Figure 6.3   Corporate learning centre project plan

Course syllabus

Distribute a syllabus on the theme 'a guide to corporate learning centre courses' to every employee in your organization. The syllabus should also be accessible on the intranet. The syllabus should be user-friendly and kept up to date, listing under subject areas all the courses available in the corporate learning centre. It should also contain an introduction to the concept of open learning, and give instructions on booking a course and the centre's exact location.

Course catalogue

A more comprehensive course catalogue should be prepared for managers for reference. This may also be made available over the intranet. Each course is allocated a page in the catalogue, giving subject group, course code, title, learning objectives, course content, duration, delivery system, equipment required for the courseware, and in the case of e-learning, a password for access.

Public relations

Write an article about the launch for your local newspaper and the company newsletter. Local radio stations should be informed about the event. Specialist computer and educational magazines could be targeted. The idea is to create as much publicity and interest in the corporate learning centre as possible. This is also very good publicity generally for your company, particularly as a provider of state-of-the-art training and development procedures.

Official launch

Most launches take place after work or during lunch hour, even though it might be better to hold it during working hours as a sign of commitment to staff training and development. The chief executive of your organization will carry out the official launch, and give an address on the vision, mission and role of the corporate learning centres in training and development, and their contribution to business needs, corporate objectives and the personal development of individuals. This address should be followed by a reception with wine and refreshments. Guided tours of the centre and demonstrations of courseware and Internet-based e-learning programmes should be provided for those interested in seeing the facilities available.

Sales promotion during the launch

Use the launch as an opportunity for an in-house sales promotion campaign, using noticeboards, e-mail, in-house journals such as company and departmental newsletters, posters, and the internal postal system to distribute newsletters and brochures.

Presentations

Live presentations on corporate learning centres will arouse the interest of departments, work stations, participation councils and interested employees. Employees will not just flock into the corporate learning centre when it opens. They must be made aware of how they will benefit from open learning.

External use

Guided tours around the corporate learning centre should be available for groups from inside and outside the organization on request. As soon as the novelty wears off, numbers using the centre are bound to fall. It might be a good idea to open the centre's facilities to children and relatives of staff and outside companies on a fee-paying basis to keep the capacity of the centre fully occupied. Small organizations which do not themselves have the resources to finance a corporate learning centre may wish to use its services. Clarify any copyright issues on the centre's courseware within the centre with the original producer before you do this.

Marketing before and after the launch

Marketing must be on a continuous basis, to maintain custom and interest. If you don't market the corporate learning centre, it will become under-utilized and the expensive equipment will slowly gather dust.

Corporate learning centre newsletter

Interest is renewed through advertising and sales promotion in a corporate learning centre newsletter on a monthly or bi-monthly basis. Brochures and e-mail may also be used to advise of new courses and to target particular individuals and categories of employees.

The company newsletter can highlight success stories about employees who have just completed a corporate learning centre programme, their feedback on the programme, and how they applied it to their work.

People like to be treated as winners, so this type of publicity will encourage further bookings. It could also include articles on learning centres in other organizations.

The newsletter may be produced cheaply in-house by the co-ordinator using a desktop publishing package. Contents may include reviews of new and popular courses, tips on learning skills, and advances in education technology such as e-learning. The internal noticeboard could be used for special promotional displays, but a special corporate learning centre noticeboard placed at strategic locations throughout the company is probably the best option, as there is often fierce competition from other departments for space on internal noticeboards.

Summary

Corporate learning centres should be located where there are high concentrations of employees, and where they are easily accessible and highly visible. A reception area is needed for counselling, course appraisal, administration, course enquiries and storage of learning materials. The booths may be dedicated to particular equipment and specified subject courseware. The environment should offer the right mood and atmosphere for learners.

Market research is carried out to establish the likely demand for a corporate learning centre. If this is favourable, then an official launch can be planned and implemented. An in-house sales promotion campaign should be undertaken using noticeboards, e-mail, in-house journals and posters. Marketing is not only needed at the launch stage, but also on a continuous basis to maintain custom and interest. An up-to-date catalogue of corporate learning centre courseware and e-learning programmes is necessary. Technical support is essential if the centre is run smoothly. A trained co-ordinator will be able to diagnose and solve routine problems.

7 The media used in corporate learning centres

Introduction

The media used in corporate learning centres include CD-ROM/DVD, e-learning programmes, audio, CD, video, the Internet and e-mail, and of course books and workbooks.

Compact Disc – Read Only Memory (CD-ROM)

CD-ROM is one of the most cost-effective training media. It emerged in the early 1990s as the preferred tool for technology-based training. It provides an interactive multimedia learning experience between a learner and a computer in which the computer provides the majority of the stimulus, the learner responds, and the computer analyses the response and provides learner feedback. The material should be user-friendly, interactive, and provide knowledge of results.

Because of the improved graphics capabilities of PCs, CD-ROM courses are now of a high standard with clear learning objectives, colour, graphics, high interaction and video sequences. They have come a long way from CBT courses on 3.5-inch discs, which in many cases were literally books on disks, with the minimum of interaction.

The one-to-one nature of CD-ROM makes it possible to monitor learner understanding constantly. A well-designed programme will respond immediately based on the needs of the individual learner, and will

Media	Strengths	Weaknesses	Subjects	Ability to hold
E-learning	Accessibility JIT learning Self-paced	Not suitable for soft skills Not suitable for craft skills	Wide choice of courses available	Very good
DVD	Same as CD-ROM, but greater capacity	Will eventually be replaced by online e-learning	Increasing range available	Good
CD-ROM	Images Sound Large capacity	Will be replaced by DVD	Wide range available	Good
Audio/CDs	Flexible Inexpensive	No images Passive No feedback	Most topics Management audios	Poor
Video/DVD	Images Sound	Passive No feedback	All topics	Good
Text	Portable Inexpensive	Little interaction	All topics	Poor

Figure 7.1 Media used in corporate learning centres

maintain a log of progress. CD-ROM courseware is inexpensive to reproduce and distribute. In a networked situation, CD-ROMs may be accessed through the company's intranet.

CD-ROM multimedia courses are generally rated very highly by users. The discs look exactly like the CD discs you have in your home stereo, but are formatted for computer data rather than sound. They provide the cheapest form of storage device, with a storage capacity equivalent to about 500 floppy discs. You can store about 250 000 pages on each disc, which is the equivalent of 500 books. Remember the 32 volumes of the *Encyclopedia Britannica*, and compare them with the two CD-ROMs that have taken their place. Better still, you can now access these volumes on the Internet. CD-ROM provides access to very large information banks, with text, colour, graphics, high-quality still images and some moving pictures with high-quality sound.

The CD-ROM player may be a separate unit linked to the PC, but in modern PCs it is almost always a built-in feature of the PC. This demonstrates the confidence that the computer industry has in the future of the CD-ROM. However, it is likely that over the next five years, online e-learning will become the preferred technology-based training medium, and will replace CD-ROMs. The term 'multimedia' is now taken to mean the CD-ROM/DVD as the delivery mechanism.

CD-ROM training courseware is available for *Microsoft Office*, *WordPerfect*, *PowerPoint* and *Microsoft Word*, as well as introductions to PCs and the Internet. Human resource development skills are also covered on CD-ROM, with programmes on project management, leadership, motivation, time management, presentation and writing skills. Operational management areas such as statistical process control and total quality management are also catered for.

Hall (2001) reports that Domino's Pizza, Inc. has developed CD-ROM-based training on a variety of topics for employees at its franchises, such as customer service, marketing, management development, profitability and hiring. Since each franchise owns its own computer system, CD-ROM was the preferred option because of platform compatibility and Internet access issues. However, this could change in the future.

Education

There is now a new range of software which blends the advanced graphics and slick presentation of top-selling games with solid educational experiences. These are known as 'Edutainment' packages, and cover a broad range of subjects. They are aimed at children aged four and up. Examples include Microsoft's *Encarta* and Microsoft's *Musical Instruments*. *Encarta* is a complete encyclopaedia on CD-ROM or DVD. Its great advantage over conventional encyclopaedias is that it combines sound, text, graphics and video – which, of course, adds to its overall appeal and educational value. Microsoft's *Musical Instruments* has topics ranging from the accordion to the zurna. It is divided into four broad sections – families of instruments, instruments of the world, an A to Z of instruments, and music ensembles. These are discovery learning packages, and put fun back into learning, where it should be. There are also CD-ROM/DVD packages on history, geography, science, medicine, the human body and other educational topics.

Because of the vastly superior capabilities of the CD-ROM and DVD, they have superseded the 3.5-inch CBT disk and interactive video (IV) as the major courseware medium in corporate learning centres. The Open University uses CD-ROM extensively on its courses. Modern PCs include a CD-ROM/DVD drive as a standard feature.

Digital Versatile Disk (DVD)

This is an enhanced CD-ROM format capable of storing up to a maximum of 17GB of data (enough for a full-length feature film). DVD has 25 times the storage capacity of CD-ROM, and handles video, audio and data in one format. This format is expected to eventually replace current CD-ROM drives in computers, as well as VHS videotapes and laserdiscs. DVD players are downward-compatible with existing CD-ROMs. Most new PCs now come with DVD drives as standard. This means you can play DVD movies or use software sold on DVD format, such as encyclopaedias.

Audiotapes/Compact Discs (CDs)

Audiotapes have proved quite popular with corporate learning centre users. Many learners use the loan service and listen to tapes at home in their own time. They can be listened to in the car while commuting to and from work, and because of this have proven very popular. Why not use this time to increase your education in management, personal development, languages and so on? Think of all the subject areas you could become expert in if you used this time productively. Many people spend up to two hours or more each day commuting to and from work – about ten hours a week, or up to 460 hours per typical working year. In a few years you could study the equivalent of a university degree programme while commuting to work, in your car or by public transport.

You can listen to and replay the material, as often as you like. You can stop the tape anywhere you wish and repeat any parts until you're happy that you really understand the points. In a lecture situation, it is not possible to do this. Audiotapes are very good for learners who are not too fond of reading.

Some people find it very difficult to concentrate on the spoken word for long periods. This can be overcome to a certain extent by stopping the cassette player every ten minutes or so and summarizing key points to date. Better still, create a Mind Map® of the audio as you listen. At the end you will have completed a comprehensive Mind Map® which you can use to review the topic in the future. Some audio programmes come complete with workbooks, exercises and projects to provide the necessary amount of interaction to help learning. CDs, because of their superior sound quality, flexibility and durability, are slowly replacing audiotapes.

Videotapes

A picture speaks more than a thousand words, and moving pictures with sound add an extra dimension. Many videotape programmes are accompanied by workbooks which facilitate interaction with the material. Video programmes are particularly suitable for language training, and a wide range are available.

There are a good variety of suppliers who produce high-quality management videos aimed at supervisory, management and professional people. There are also a wide range of videos available on information technology and other technical subjects. Videotapes will eventually be replaced by DVD.

The Internet and e-mail

The Internet is a labyrinth of academic, commercial, government and military computer networks that are interconnected. It was started in 1969 as an experimental network by the US Department of Defense. One of its original objectives was to enable scientists working on government projects to communicate with each other.

The experiment started by connecting four computers. Now the Internet connects more than 45 000 computer networks in government, education, business, military and consumer areas, in more than seventy countries. Each network can support anywhere from a few to thousands of users. *Internet Business News* (5 October 2000) reports that there are 30 million registered domain names on the Internet, and predicts this will reach 60 million before 2003. In 2001, it was estimated that more than 400 million people use the Web each day.

Access to the Internet provides a useful resource to secondary and tertiary-level students. It suggests all sorts of possibilities, especially for distance learning. For example, the BBC's Website (<http://www.bbc.co.uk/education>) is a good source of general e-learning opportunities. The technology is now there to enable learners in different organizations anywhere in the world to link up with each other and share knowledge and experience. This is a type of self-directed learning. Multinational companies, for example, will have learners from different countries following the same course and supported by the same tutor, with whom they can communicate via video and audio conferencing and e-mail. Rosenberg (2001) reports that Delta Airlines and Ford have given computers and Internet access to all their employees.

The global village is now on our doorsteps. Today, people can search thousands of databases and libraries on the Internet, browse through hundreds of millions of documents, journals, books and computer programmes, and keep up to date with news, business, sports and weather reports.

Jones (1998) reports that the Open University is treating the Internet cautiously. It doesn't believe the World Wide Web provides the complete answer to distance learning. In 25 years, it has learnt that there is no magic single learning medium. The Web will be integrated into its multimedia learning system. However, it will not be moving all teaching and learning onto the Web.

E-mail is one of the most widely used features of the Internet. Large businesses have used e-mail for years, enabling employees to send messages, memos, files and reports to each other. But in the past, most e-mail systems only worked within single organizations. The advantage of linking into the Internet is that you can send e-mail to other organizations. E-mail and corporate Websites can be used to market the corporate learning centre not only to your own employees but to outside businesses as well. E-mail can be used to facilitate collaborative learning in e-learning programmes. Universities use e-mail as one of the channels of communication between students and lecturers in their distance learning programmes.

Littlefield (1994) reports that Edinburgh's Telford College is developing innovative forms of open learning using e-mail. It uses this medium to run a course for students in Denmark who are studying for a Scottish Vocational Qualification in communication studies. They are also looking for EU funding to run an English-language course for people in remote parts of Europe where they can communicate with Edinburgh using British Telecom's new £3000 PC-based videophone.

E-learning

E-learning refers to training delivered by a PC via the Internet or intranet. Some programmes are designed so that learners can take them at their own pace, while others take place in real time, as virtual training courses. In most organizations, learning centres will form an important part of e-learning delivery. Dunn (2001) reports that in the UK, well-established providers like Xebec and EPIC, and large organizations such as the banks and building societies are well into their second decade of producing or using e-learning programmes.

E-learning is part of the learning mix in a blended learning approach.

Masie (2002a) maintains that some of the most successful implementations of e-learning have started with a blended learning approach. Learners who have doubts about the effectiveness of e-learning often find blended learning very acceptable. One major financial service company used blended learning for one year, prior to offering any solo online classes, to help its staff get used to the new format. Instructor-led training, on-the-job training, books, videos, audiotapes, CDs and CD-ROMs are other parts of the learning mix.

Compared with CD-ROM, Internet-based learning is more convenient, there is access to a wider choice of courses, and learning management systems provide timetabling and reporting features. E-learning programmes may cost as little as £100 or as much as £4000, depending on the length and depth of the course.

Developing and hosting e-learning programmes internally gives companies complete control of content, but can be very expensive. This may only be viable for companies with a high volume of training, and scope for economies of scale. It may be easier and more cost-effective to allow employees to access Internet-based e-learning programmes offered by outside suppliers. It is not essential to have an intranet to make e-learning accessible to employees.

Dunn (2001) reports that corporate universities provide an ideal basis on which to build e-learning. Motorola University, available throughout its organization in Europe, is moving much of its training online, with the objective of getting up to 50 per cent online by 2005. The University for Lloyds TSB, PricewaterhouseCoopers e-cademie, and the BT Internet College are all going in a similar direction.

Sloman (2001) reports that the Virtual Business School was launched in October 1998 by Ernst & Young's management consultancy. Among the programmes available to its staff are leadership development and an MBA. He also reports that in the summer of 2001, Harvard Business School Publishing launched High Performance Management On-Line, which is an intranet/Internet tool using multimedia technology to offer interactive case studies. A number of *Harvard Business Review* articles are built in as a resource library. Subjects covered include exercising power and influence, managing change, and stress management.

Sloman (2001) also reports that in 1999 an IPD-sponsored survey revealed that a quarter of all respondents were using the Internet or intranet to train staff. Since then, that number has grown, and will continue to do so.

Benefits of e-learning

Survey results

A study by e-learning magazine (<http://www.elearningmag.com>) indicates that 79 per cent of users feel that the principle advantage to online e-learning is that learners can access courses on their computers wherever they are and whenever they want. Fifty-nine per cent say it allows for self-paced learning and saves money. Fifty per cent say it provides 'just-in-time' learning, while one-third like the ease of use, fast distribution, and how easy it is to change content (*Business Wire*, 25 July 2002). E-learning brings us closer to the just-enough, just-in-time, and just-for-me paradigm. Employees want quick just-in-time training, and want to know how it will help them to do their jobs more effectively.

Learners

People who are computer-literate, university educated and used to learning and teaching themselves are particularly suited to e-learning. Others need training, plenty of encouragement, and inducements to start.

It is estimated that 97 per cent of learners need human support. E-learning provides trainers with the opportunity to become online mentors by using e-mail, tutor support, reference links, bulletin boards and discussion groups.

E-learning enables learners to take responsibility for their own learning, and ensure that the learning is relevant to their particular needs. They are no longer passive recipients of information, but can actively manage their own learning.

Access

Live e-learning enables people from anywhere in the world to access learning and discourse with each other. It has been used successfully in sales training, but does need the services of a trainer. Kearsley (2002) reports that participants conduct their training online through their own Internet connections. After registering, the learner is addressed personally, and all communications are transmitted through the personal e-mail system. Quality interactive materials are provided which require learners to submit exercises and comments. Each sales group has an online facilitator or tutor. After submitting exercises, there is an opportunity for the facilitator to comment and suggest alternative approaches. The learner can contact the facilitator at any time during the programme.

Because e-learning lends itself to knowledge-based training, it is perfectly suited to accountancy, health and safety, industrial relations or any other profession that requires a great deal of compliance and regulatory knowledge. As products and legislation grow ever more complicated, it helps to have an online inventory of things that people should know.

E-learning provides access to experts who otherwise might be too expensive to bring in to the company.

Davies (2001) reports that Interwise is an example of a online e-learning product that facilitates the use of *PowerPoint*, allowing users to collaborate on an electronic whiteboard. It can send text notes to the lecturer and other participants, launch tests and surveys, break up the group into smaller workgroups for discussion, and question the instructor and other learners.

Efficiency

Hall (2002) reports that students who are particularly advanced in a topic can skip material and concentrate on the challenging parts, and thus prevent boredom. In the case of students with a physical disability, e-learning can make learning more accessible.

Enhanced administration, assessment and management of learners through a learning management system means that some organizations use e-learning to test knowledge before staff attend classroom training.

Elimination of the need for physical resources makes it likely that online e-learning programmes will eventually make CD-ROMs obsolete.

Both time spent in training and travel costs are reduced significantly. Masie (2002b) reports that a manufacturing company recently transformed a week-long safety programme into a three-part offering: a one-day classroom session, multiple online lessons and simulations, and a final one-day discussion and exam session. Learners don't attend the final day until they have accomplished the online work. This has resulted in higher success rates, fewer hours away from the job, and greater learner transfer of content to the workplace.

The number of employees trained is significantly higher, and each receives the same message.

Time off work for training is reduced.

E-learning can be used to prepare learners before instructor-led training, and to reinforce their learning after it. This reduces the amount of time needed for classroom training. Pope (2002) reports that the increased ability to share best practice across different parts of an organization is a major benefit of e-learning. On acquisition, global companies can help integrate a new business by quickly sharing cultural, technical and procedural information. Retaining intellectual capital can also be achieved by integrating knowledge management systems with e-learning.

E-learning is easily updated, and can be distributed quickly to all employees.

Limitations of e-learning

Usage

Sloman (2001) reports that Xebec McGraw-Hill's 2000 survey showed that 80 per cent of organizations have a corporate intranet. However, less than 30 per cent were using it to deliver online training, and only 39 per cent of those rated it successful. Nevertheless, almost 80 per cent of all respondents believed that online learning will ultimately prove successful.

Online learning hasn't lived up to the hype of 'the end of the classroom as we know it'. This hasn't happened and is unlikely to happen. Hall (2001) reports that many organizations, including IBM, Ernst & Young, and Verizon Communications, use a 'blended' approach, combining online courses with 'live' training. Rosenberg (2001) reports that when Dell Learning, the Dell Corporation's training organization, releases a new programme or tool on the Web, sometimes it is introduced in a non-threatening classroom situation, to help people feel more comfortable with it. This results in higher levels of use on the job.

Acceptability

Generic programmes may not win acceptance. A significant investment in time is required to develop bespoke e-learning programmes.

There is still a perception that certification from a 'bricks and mortar' training organization is more credible than from a virtual university or e-learning company.

Suitability

It is most suitable for IT- and knowledge-based subjects. 'Soft' skills are still best learnt in the training room. Team-building, coaching, influencing skills, social networking and building culture require physical presence for optimal learning.

Complex psychomotor and craft skills cannot be taught with a mouse and keyboard. Simulation technology is still mostly inadequate for this purpose.

Completion

Islam (2002) reports that according to Forrester Research (<http://www.forrester.com>), 70 per cent of those who start an e-learning course never complete it. Some people prefer to learn through social interaction, while others are reluctant to take on the responsibility for their own learning. Moshinskie (2001) reports that Motorola University found that a significant gap existed between the number of employees who had registered for online courses and those who actually finished them.

Shepherd (2001a) reports that in a research study conducted by Corporate University Xchange, corporate e-learners said that their main reason for dropping out was lack of time. They had difficulty working from their desktops because of frequent interruptions, and couldn't always get access to the course materials over the Internet while working from home. Hall (2001) writes that Rockwell Collins addressed this issue by building geographically dispersed learning centres where people could go to learn. According to research by ASTD and the Masie centre, 76 per cent of e-learners said they preferred to take courses during working hours. The report recommends strongly that companies provide employees with time and space to learn in company time.

Culture

Many companies treat e-learning as a project, rather than a process requiring ongoing commitment.

The organizational culture may not support e-learning. Learning is seen as a cost and waste of time, rather than an investment.

Many companies see e-learning solely as an investment in technology, rather than as a means to meet identified training and business needs.

Cost

Prickett (2002) reports that Fathom (an e-learning programme) cost Columbia University nearly $20 million without finding an audience. UNext spent at least $115 million without bringing much to market, even though it developed the core business curriculum with some of the world's leading academic institutions, including the London School of Economics.

High costs and the lack of a cheap broadband infrastructure are still hampering the quality of e-learning programmes. The driving force behind most companies' investment in e-learning is cost saving. However, it is very expensive to develop and deliver. Cost savings are only achieved by very big organizations with large number of learners through economies of scale. Lamb (2002) reports that most users are multinational companies with more than 5000 employees.

Design

Many e-learning programmes are badly designed, with little adherence to learning principles. They often provide quick answers, rather than encouraging reflective learning. Bad instructional design equates with poor learning. Problems learners encounter include long download waits, choppy video, poor navigation structure, lack of or inappropriate graphics and animation, inadequate interaction, and content that lacks chunking. Generic products are based on the 'one size fits all' principle, and these may not exactly match particular business and learner needs.

Enright (2002) reports that there hasn't been any real serious analysis of the learning effectiveness of virtual education, and that we mostly take a leap of faith in this regard. In addition, he is concerned that vendors are often less concerned about improving the quality and accessibility of education than making money.

Geisman (2001) reports that Forrester Research identified the three most common obstacles to a successful e-learning strategy as: lack of interactivity (56 per cent), cultural resistance (41 per cent), and lack of bandwidth (36 per cent). Vaughan Frazee (2001) reports that executives of EarthLink.com suggest at least three factors that keep people from adopting Internet technology: lack of money, a fear of technology, and a lack of understanding of the technology's value.

Human factor

Many people lack the self-reliant skills needed to be successful e-learners. They are not always good at using support systems, knowledge management systems, and collaborating online with instructors and other learners.

Unlike traditional instructor-led training, with e-learning you can't look students in the eye, talk to them at the break, and get direct feedback on whether they're really learning.

Many workers spend a significant part of their working day in front of computer monitors, so may be disinclined to spend more time in front of their monitors studying e-learning programmes.

Evaluating e-learning courses

Questions to consider include:

- Is the course structure logical, complete and comprehensive?
- What learning support is available – online mentoring or learning communities?
- Can learners do their job more effectively as a result of completing the course?

- Does the course have clear objectives, and is it clear what will be learned and why it is important to learn it?
- How will the learner know that the learning has been achieved?
- Are the courses user-friendly, engaging, interactive and easy to navigate?
- Do the courses have good instructional design in line with sound learning principles, and do they meet your training and business needs?
- Are the courses capable of customization, and if so, what are the cost implications?
- How often are courses updated?
- Can you replace courses because of poor demand or changing business needs?
- Are the courses compatible with your existing learning management system?
- Can the courses be blended with more traditional forms of training?

Text-based courses

With all the emphasis on technology, we should not forget the humble book. Bates (1988) says that while technology can bring many benefits to open learning, in most cases it is not a cheap option, and needs to be used with care and skill. For this reason, established media such as print have an important role to play in open learning. Indeed, books offer most of the advantages of computer-based training, such as accessibility and flexibility, without the cost of expensive hardware and software, and have the added advantage of being very portable and not subject to breakdown. In fact, a lot of courseware is accompanied by manuals. Books, like courseware, provide content expertise. Courseware is usually more attractive and easier to learn, but books can also be made user-friendly.

Jones (1998) reports that Open University students prefer printed paper as the main vehicle for study texts. They do not like reading a lot of material off the screen. This is partly because OU students study on the move – in commuter trains, in aeroplanes, and in hotels. Text is still more convenient in these situations. In addition, computer monitors cause greater eyestrain and fatigue.

With the greater awareness of learning theory, and the arrival of desktop publishing, the quality, design and layout of books have improved dramatically in the last few years. Chapters now often start with learning objectives and overviews, and conclude with summaries – the old 'tell 'em what you're going to tell 'em, and then tell 'em what you've told 'em' principle put into practice. The design, quality of illustrations, layout and typography have also advanced considerably. So nowadays, books are usually well written, and are easier to read and understand.

Magazines and journals

The corporate learning centre should stock a suitable range of magazines and journals aimed at the learners. Reading magazines, and indeed good-quality newspapers, probably offers the best way of keeping up to date. The type of magazines will be determined by the type of employees the centre services. A typical range might include management, marketing, business, accountancy, information technology and technical and engineering journals.

Summary

CD-ROM is one of the most cost-effective training media. CD-ROM offers an interactive learning experience between a learner and a computer in which the computer provides the majority of the stimulus, the learner responds, and the computer analyses the response and provides learner feedback. CD-ROM and DVD multimedia courses are generally rated very highly by users. CD-ROM discs look exactly like the CD discs you have in your home stereo, but are formatted for computer data rather than sound. DVD is similar to CD-ROM, but has greater storage capacity.

Audiotapes and CDs are very popular with corporate learning centre users, as they can be listened to in the learner's own time and while commuting to and from work. Videotapes are popular for a similar reason, because they can be viewed at home.

E-mail and e-learning are some of the most widely used features of the Internet, and are now used extensively by many organizations. There are now a huge variety of Internet-based e-learning programmes available. The benefits and limitations of e-learning were discussed. Questions to consider when choosing an e-learning programme were posed. Organizations can be connected to each other by using the Internet.

With all the emphasis on technology, the humble book should not be forgotten. It can still play an important role in any corporate learning centre.

8 Management and administration

Introduction

This chapter examines the role of the co-ordinator, and the administration and management of a corporate learning centre. Housekeeping, security, administration, health and safety and the role of the co-ordinator as tutor will be explored. The need for the support of mentors are also discussed.

Organization

The organization of a corporate learning centre can range from a centralized to a decentralized structure. Centralization offers economies of scale, but may become bureaucratic and inflexible. Decentralization encourages initiative and flexibility, but may incur some duplication of resources.

The best organization structure centre depends on the circumstances in the company. Even with decentralization and corporate learning centres under the control of local management, it will still be necessary to have a strong functional influence from the Training and Development department.

Questions of mission, vision, policy, finance and budgets, design and location, purchase of courseware and equipment, subscription to e-learning programmes, staffing and administration, management and reporting arrangements must all be thought out very clearly. Logistical, tactical and strategic plans should be drawn up and linked in to the training and development plan, and ultimately to the formal corporate planning process of the company. Planning presumes objectives, targets and budgets, and control involves comparing actual results with targets and taking of corrective action to put the actual activities of the corporate learning centre back on target again.

Co-ordinator's person specification

A corporate learning centre co-ordinator needs to possess all-round skills:

- able to work intensively for long periods under demanding conditions
- good appearance
- recognized qualification in information technology
- experience in training and open learning
- good problem-solving and diagnostic skills
- good customer relations
- good telephone voice and manner
- good administration skills
- selling and marketing skills
- good hands-on information technology skills
- Internet, desktop publishing, graphical and spreadsheet skills
- interested in keeping up to date with computer-based training, including e-learning
- a self-developer
- experience in training and development
- solving learning needs of employees
- self-starter
- capable of accepting responsibility
- able to handle demands of numerous customers simultaneously
- capable of withstanding pressure
- friendly and extrovert
- willing to work flexible hours if necessary.

In general, co-ordinators must have a good personality, and an interest in training and development and the learning needs of employees. They must enjoy meeting people and solving their training needs. Listening, empathizing, coaching, counselling and tutoring skills are all necessary for the job. They must have a sympathetic ear for the concerns and problems of employees.

Co-ordinator's job description

The co-ordinator's job will involve the following:

- day-to-day administration and management of the corporate learning centre
- promoting and marketing corporate learning centre courseware, including e-learning programmes
- operating the learning management system
- liaising with suppliers of hardware and software
- drawing up and agreeing the budget for the centre
- generally assisting learners as necessary
- operating and controlling the home loan library system for audios, CDs, videos and text
- ensuring that the centre is kept tidy and clean
- ensuring that copyright is not infringed
- maintaining stationery stocks for the centre
- selecting and purchasing courseware and equipment
- certifying invoices and passing them on to accounts for payment
- devising and agreeing costing and pricing systems
- keeping up to date on computer-based training and e-learning programmes
- coding new items, and keeping the catalogue and course syllabus up to date
- issuing a monthly or quarterly corporate learning centre newsletter
- showing visitors around the centre as required
- carrying out a virus security check each morning
- having hands-on familiarity with the major courseware in the centre
- carrying out routine problem-solving and equipment maintenance
- ensuring that learners fill out evaluation of courseware forms on completion of courses
- maintaining contact with managers regarding their requirements for corporate learning courses
- carrying out occasional surveys to get feedback from users on the quality of the corporate learning centre's courses and service
- producing statistics on usage of the centre as required.

Co-ordinators must be familiar with the major courseware stocked in the corporate learning centre and e-learning programmes accessible from the centre. They can use any spare time to acquire this expertise. They can also advise on the content, standard and duration of the programme. Co-ordinators cannot be subject experts on everything, but over a period of time they can acquire a fair amount of expertise in many areas by studying subject courseware and e-learning programmes for which there is a good demand. However, they may recommend subject matter experts or specialists elsewhere in the organization. This can be organized via e-mail, the telephone or tutorials.

Course guide

The co-ordinator must ensure that the course guide is kept up to date. Each course is recorded under four headings: code number, title, type (audio, CD, video, text, CD-ROM/DVD and e-learning) and duration in hours. New courses need to be added, and old courses, and those courses no longer in demand, should be withdrawn. Updates or reprints of the guide should be carried out annually.

Computer security and virus protection

The co-ordinator will switch on the computers each morning and operate the virus-checking software. A virus could be introduced into the system by learners using discs from outside. It is important that this risk is safeguarded against, and that the integrity of the systems is maintained. The virus-checking software must be kept up to date. To prevent contamination by virus, software should not be loaned out from the centre. CD-ROM/DVD courses should be studied in the centre only under the supervision of the co-ordinator.

Copyright

Computer software is protected by copyright law, and to a lesser extent, by patent law. Copyright protects the expression of the idea, but not the idea itself. The form is protected, not the idea. Reproduction of a programme is an infringement of the rightholder's copyright. This applies to print, video, audio, illustrations, photographs, computer software and broadcast programmes. There are some legal concessions for education and training if the material is used in-house and not for commercial gain. However, always get copyright permission if you want to reproduce illustrations.

Unauthorized copying of software, audio or video programmes is illegal unless the user has permission or a licence to do so. A company may be liable for damages if its employees infringe copyright. Apart from the vigilance of the co-ordinator, periodic checks by the company's internal auditors will act as a deterrent.

The corporate learning centre co-ordinator must not allow breach of copyright. Learners should not be allowed to copy materials in the learning centre for their private use. It might also be the policy of the corporate learning centre not to loan discs or videos to learners in case of breach of copyright or introduction of viruses into the system. A licence may be obtained from the owner to make multiple copies of a programme if the company feels there is sufficient demand. Many software and video programmes are now protected to prevent unauthorized copying. If in doubt, always consult the original producer of the material.

Bookings and preparation

The co-ordinator will review bookings for the day, enter them on the learning management system, and record bookings that have been taken up on the previous day. Learners should be advised to book in advance, as they may be disappointed if they just turn up on the day and the particular booth is already booked. Likewise, they should also give adequate notice of cancellations so that other learners are not prevented from using the booth at that time. A strict policy must be operated in this regard. Learners who fail to give advance notice of cancellations should be reminded that this is unacceptable. Courseware should be pre-loaded on the machines and be menu-driven, so that everything is ready for the learner on arrival.

Information and feedback

At the start of each week, the co-ordinator should provide information to management on usage of the corporate learning centre for the previous week. This information will identify who is using the centre and the type of courses that are in high demand. In the case of multiple sites, comparative usage statistics should be prepared. An inter-centre league table could be compiled, and the reasons for differences investigated.

Course evaluation sheets should be issued to learners and completed evaluation forms returned to the co-ordinator before the learner leaves the centre. Feedback on e-learning will be provided on line. This feedback will help validate courses for quality, relevance, user-friendliness, design and timeliness (up to date). Courses with consistently poor feedback should be withdrawn and replaced with better-quality programmes. This feedback, where relevant, should also be supplied to producers, to help them upgrade their courses.

Stock management

Keep a record of all issues and returns of books, audiotapes, CDs and videos. Where a personal and postal loan system is in operation, a vigorous follow-up system will ensure that loaned material is returned promptly, and will prevent other clients waiting unnecessarily. It may be the policy of the corporate learning centre to insist that clients must replace lost items, but this rule should be applied with discretion. An up-to-date inventory of books, audiotapes, CDs and videos will ensure that all stock is accounted for.

Courseware acquisition

The co-ordinator may be responsible for purchasing and evaluating courseware. Courseware may date quickly or suffer damage through repeated use, and so should be upgraded or replaced as necessary. This may be carried out in conjunction with subject experts and the Training and Development department, which should ensure adherence to corporate training policy and avoid duplication of effort. There must be good reasons for booking employees onto external courses if the equivalent course is available in the corporate learning centre.

Equipment purchase and maintenance

An experienced co-ordinator should be able to make most purchasing decisions without recourse to third parties. Large companies with many corporate learning centres may employ specialist staff to purchase courseware or evaluate e-learning programmes. Equipment must be maintained, upgraded and replaced. Maintenance contracts can be placed with equipment suppliers. They must be able to offer a helpline for routine problems, and respond quickly when equipment breaks down.

Personal skills

The co-ordinator must have a friendly and helpful telephone manner. Bookings may be made in person or on the phone, and the co-ordinator should build up a good relationship with clients. Being friendly, listening with empathy, and remembering and using client's names are important skills for the co-ordinator to develop. As well as attracting new customers, they have to build and maintain loyalty among existing customers.

Absence

An important aspect of administration is providing cover when the co-ordinator is on holiday, sick leave or attending a training course. Most of this absence can be planned for, with the exception of sick leave, and cover must be provided. The 'relief' must be trained to take over the duties of the co-ordinator smoothly, and should be available at short notice in case of emergencies.

Housekeeping

The co-ordinator will liaise with the cleaners so that the corporate learning centre is part of their daily cleaning roster. The co-ordinator should also ensure that the centre is tidy, and that computer keyboards and screens, headphones and discs are kept clean. The head on the video recorder must always be clean. For hygiene reasons, headphones should be disinfected occasionally to guard against the possibility of ear infections.

Security

Security and control are an important aspect of the co-ordinator's job. Courseware should be kept under lock and key and issued under the control and watchful eye of the co-ordinator, to prevent unauthorized tampering and copying. Remember, the company is responsible for employee infringement of copyright. An inventory of courseware and hardware should be taken on a regular basis to ensure that everything is controlled and accounted for. An inventory of hardware may be displayed on the wall of the corporate learning centre. The items stocked in the centre are valuable and easily transportable, and should be protected from theft or damage.

The corporate learning centre should be staffed during the day. At other times, access should only be for authorized staff, with swipecard or similar security. All software packages, including videos, audiotapes, CDs, and books, should be locked away in glass display cabinets and under the control of the co-ordinator.

Data protection

All organizations which store data on individuals should be aware of their legal duties. Under the Data Protection Act, individuals have a right to know who is keeping information about them on computer files. They are entitled to be told the purpose for any information held, and its type. Computer users must comply with a series of data protection principles, which include acquiring data 'fairly', and keeping it accurate and up to date. Personal data should be adequate, relevant and not excessive for its purpose, and should be secured against unauthorized access.

Health and safety

The co-ordinator has general responsibility for the health and safety of clients while they are using the learning centre. Potential dangers to look for include trailing wires, unsecured bookshelves, slippery floors, courseware left on passageways and so on. Good housekeeping and tidiness will prevent any safety problems from arising. Static electricity may be a problem where there are screens and carpets in a confined area. Antistatic sprays can deal with the problem.

The co-ordinator should be aware of potential health problems caused by prolonged use of VDUs, some of which relate to matters of safety. Symptoms include headaches, backaches, sore finger joints, fatigue and tired eyes. Further information is available in the leaflet entitled 'Working with VDUs' issued by the UK Health and Safety Executive.

Continuous working in front of a VDU may cause fatigue. The co-ordinator should advise learners to take breaks every half hour or so. There have been several studies on whether working with a VDU can affect an operator's eyesight. None of them has found any evidence to link VDUs with damage to the eyes, or to making existing eye defects worse. In any event, all the VDUs in the corporate learning centre should be fitted with a glare protection screen.

The co-ordinator should ensure that learners are comfortably seated and that the learning centre is well lit and quiet, to minimize the risk of headaches, backaches or eyestrain. The chairs should have adjustable height and back support, and the desks should be of an appropriate height. Good posture will help prevent backache, muscle tiredness and discomfort in the arms, shoulders and neck.

Modern systems have detachable keyboards and adjustable tilt-swivel screens, and these should be positioned to suit individual needs. It is not advisable for clients to rest their wrists on the edge of the keyboard or desk or bend their hands up at the wrist. There should be enough space in front of each keyboard to support wrists and lower arms. They should try to keep a soft touch on the keys, and not over-stretch their fingers. Good keyboard technique is important in prolonged operation.

Encourage learners to experiment with different layouts of keyboard, screen and document holder to find the best arrangement. Each desk should be arranged so that any bright lights are not reflected on the screen. Learners should not look directly at windows or bright lights. Use curtains or blinds to cut out unwanted light.

Training needs

Various aspects of the co-ordinator's role include those of tutor, coach, counsellor, facilitator and training needs advisor. Many people will visit the corporate learning centre without any clear idea of their training needs or what open learning courses they want to study. Through a process of listening and questioning, the co-ordinator will try to identify their training needs and endeavour to match an open learning course to meet those needs. The client should agree the outcome of the course with their immediate supervisor or manager, to ensure their support.

The rationale behind a client's choice of course might include:

- upgrading or learning a new skill
- preparing them for a new job or helping them get promotion

- training in new information technology and getting an ECDL qualification
- personal interest
- supplementing studies for a formal professional or university degree
- revising a subject area or preparing for a 'live' training programme.

Learning styles

In matching the course to the client, the co-ordinator must consider not only the client's needs, but also their learning style. Some people are interested in theories and concepts, while others are more interested in the practical application of ideas. Learners may be either left-brain-dominant or right-brain-dominant. This means that some people may be analytical and rational and prefer logical and sequential learning, while others may be creative and artistic and enjoy plenty of interaction and visual learning experiences.

Does the learner prefer listening, seeing, or activity? Do they enjoy learning holistically, by considering overviews and broad concepts, or logically, by sequentially working through details? Courses that cater for a combination of these styles will be most effective. This consideration may suggest the most suitable medium for the learner – text, audio, simulations, CDs, video, CD-ROM/DVD or Internet-based e-learning programmes. The co-ordinator should encourage learners to match the complexity of any courses to their ability, experience and learning style.

Welcoming new learners

Some learners require more help than others, perhaps in drawing up learning objectives, a training plan and time schedule to meet their needs. Learners are unlikely to be as familiar as the co-ordinator with the type, range and duration of the courses available in the corporate learning centre, so the co-ordinator should share expertise with learners. A mix of courses may be needed to meet particular training needs. The co-ordinator must be supportive, rather than intrusive. Too much interference can overwhelm new learners. Shy learners may need help but be unwilling to ask. The co-ordinator must learn when to offer help and advice, and when to stay in the background.

New learners are likely to need more support than more experienced learners. Empathy, understanding, patience and a little humour are needed on the part of the tutor. A brief explanation as to how computers work and a quick introduction to the keyboard may be needed. Some people may have difficulty in operating the mouse. A little instruction in its use will help overcome their initial awkwardness and develop the right sensitivity of touch to use the mouse proficiently. The co-ordinator may give an initial demonstration of how to switch on and close down the computers, how to load the CD-ROM/DVD drive, how to access relevant courseware, how to move around the screen, and how to access e-learning programmes on the Internet or intranet. This will help ensure that new learners make the most of their time.

Encourage new learners to use demonstrations or tutorials before they tackle the courseware, and to take the keyboarding skills course and the introduction to PCs and the Internet course. A lot of courseware is now *Windows*-based, and Microsoft's introductory and advanced CD-ROM/DVD courses on *Windows* should be recommended to new learners.

The learning curve

Employees will go through a learning curve. In any new learning situation, there is an initial stage of rapid progress, a stage of slow progress, and a stage when little or no progress is made. This last stage is called the *learning plateau*, and is the point when many learners become discouraged and give up. Seemingly insurmountable problems present themselves which will only be overcome if the learner sticks to the task. This stage may prove a real test of the learner's confidence and commitment, but once overcome, the learner can progress to a higher level of expertise. During the plateau stage, the advice, support, encouragement and counselling of the tutor is most important.

The learning cycle

David Kolb described the *learning cycle*. The learning styles of activist, reflector, theorist and pragmatist are linked to the learning cycle. Activists enjoy getting things done. They tend to be reactive rather than proactive. Reflectors tend to think deeply about their experiences and consider them from different viewpoints. Theorists like to organize different facts into coherent theories. They are keen on principles, models and systems thinking. Pragmatists like to try out things to see if they work in practice.

The learning cycle highlights the importance of reflection and continuous improvement. The mnemonic DRUD will help you remember the steps involved:

- Do something.
- Reflect on it.
- Understand it and conclude.
- Do it differently.

The learning cycle and associated learning styles are illustrated in Figure 8.1.

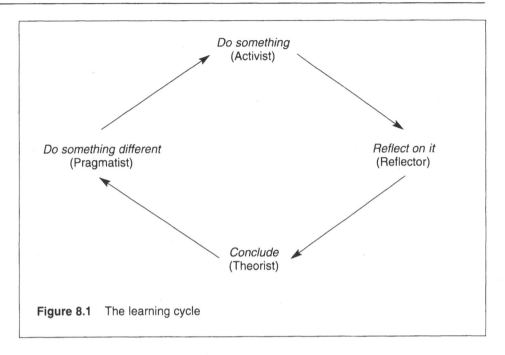

Figure 8.1   The learning cycle

It is important that corporate learning centres are designed with the learning cycle and learning styles in mind. Opportunities to do things, make mistakes, reflect on the consequences, try out new approaches and generally learn from the process should be part of the corporate learning experience.

More experienced learners

As learners use the corporate learning centre, they will become more confident and competent, and will require less support. These self-sufficient learners should be encouraged to walk in and help themselves to learning, and may act as useful advocates of the centre among new employees.

Mentor support

Mentor support is a useful aid to developing open learning. The role of the mentor is to advise, coach, coax, encourage, support, empathize with and generally assist learners. Mentors might be fellow learners, colleagues, supervisors or managers. Mentoring compensates somewhat for the problem of isolation inherent in open learning by providing human contact and a source of support and advice when needed. Online mentoring and collaborative learning is now a feature of many e-learning programmes. The decision to accept or access a mentor or other learners should rest entirely with the individuals concerned.

Irrespective of the effectiveness of self-assessment questions and exercises within courseware, they are no substitute for face-to-face feedback. Mentoring offers an opportunity to build up lasting relationships with others in the company which may be helpful to career development in the future. People learn more effectively if they receive support from trainers, tutors, managers or work colleagues, especially where the programme requires a significant commitment.

Learners who have recently completed the course may also be willing to act as mentors. They have the advantage of knowing the problems, pitfalls and anxieties of doing the course. The co-ordinator may act as a go-between to place new learners with appropriate mentors.

Meetings with mentors can be formal or informal. In a formal situation, a timetable of meetings may be agreed. In an informal situation, especially in smaller companies, people might just occasionally bump into each other in the corridor. These impromptu meetings may then be turned into opportunities for the mentor to find out how the learner is progressing, and to offer some advice and words of encouragement. This may be all the learner needs to encourage them to stick to the task. The company may also consider running workshops for people who are interested in taking on the role of mentors. These workshops explain the purpose of mentoring, how people learn, and the common problems experienced by learners.

A learning agreement between mentor and learner will set out what each expects of the other, with a timetable of learning objectives and outcomes. When the mentor is the supervisor or manager, the mentoring process may be linked to individual training plans. This helps to integrate the service provided by the corporate learning centre into the work of the company.

Study groups

Corporate learning centre users may also form study groups to meet occasionally and exchange knowledge, skills and experiences. This can be a great way of learning, getting support and making friends. Learners find it far easier to approach each other with questions than to contact a subject matter expert. Study groups will help counteract the isolation of open learning, and at the same time help members develop interpersonal skills. Online group discussion may be facilitated by e-mail, chatrooms, audio and video conferencing.

Summary

The ideal co-ordinator to run a corporate learning centre will have a certificate in information technology, a good personality with customer relations skills and an interest in education, training and development. Administration includes maintaining a course catalogue and operating a booking procedure for courses during the day. A good learning management system to facilitate this process is needed. Course evaluation should be carried out on an ongoing basis. The co-ordinator may be responsible for purchasing and evaluating courseware and e-learning programmes.

The co-ordinator should ensure that the centre is tidy and that computer keyboards and screens, headphones and discs are clean. Security and control are an important aspect of the job. The centre must be marketed creatively and continuously.

An ongoing aspect of the co-ordinator's role is that of tutor, coach, counsellor, facilitator, and training needs advisor. The co-ordinator should suit the course to the learner's needs. The learner's preferred learning style should be a consideration. In an ideal situation, mentor support would be a feature of open learning. Mentoring is particularly necessary for younger employees or for new employees in the company.

9 Marketing the corporate learning centre

Introduction

The co-ordinator should devote a significant amount of time to marketing and promotional activities. To survive in the long term, the centre must be marketed creatively and continuously. A good co-ordinator will be able to advise learners of the pros and cons of various courses and media. This is an important marketing aspect of the co-ordinator's job, and one of the ways in which new customers are identified and developed and new programmes purchased to meet the needs of learners. Other people may just drop in to see the corporate learning centre when passing by. The co-ordinator should not miss the opportunity to show them around and to encourage them to use the centre by pushing the need for lifelong learning for personal growth and career advancement.

While in the corporate learning centre, people should be encouraged to browse through the courseware in the display cabinets. These should be laid out attractively to grab attention and arouse interest. At the appropriate time, the co-ordinator may point out the advantages of particular courses, including Internet-based e-learning programmes, and name the people who have already successfully completed them. This should arouse the curiosity of the visitor, who may then be encouraged to book a corporate learning centre programme.

When a client finishes a programme, make them aware of other follow-up courses that might be of interest to them, and bring new courses to their attention. This proactive approach to selling will help to keep the usage figures high. The more employees who use the corporate learning centre, the more it becomes part of the life and culture of the organization.

Mission and vision statements

An outline of a marketing plan is shown in Figure 9.1. All good plans start with a mission statement. This sets out the purpose of the corporate learning centre, and the contribution it will make to the training and development needs of the organization. The statement should be a collaborative effort between senior management, the Training and Development department, line managers and a representative sample of staff. It is an application of the stakeholder concept, which suggests that all interested parties become involved so that they feel a sense of ownership and commitment to the centre, and will thus support it. A mission statement might be worded on the following lines:

> To provide an accessible and flexible training resource which will assist local management in the achievement of Business Objectives by linking learning to business plans and work programmes.

Vision statement

The mission statement tends to be quite broad, and sets out the basic reason for the existence of the corporate learning centre in terms of business needs and learners. The mission is supported by the vision statement, which is an inspirational mental image of the future the organization strongly desires. Vision statements should be clear, concise, easily visualized, and thus easy to remember. Who can forget the memorable mission statement from John F. Kennedy, to: 'put a man on the moon by the end of the decade'.

Part of the vision might be to provide a centre of excellence for best practice, lifelong learning and personal development. The centre should be an important means of moving towards a learning organization. The vision statement should inspire, motivate and focus the energies of learners on the achievement of learning goals. Goals tend to be more specific and measurable, and should be aligned to the vision.

The corporate learning centre vision statement should be incorporated into as many communication channels as possible including newsletters, advertising, marketing campaigns and on plaques displayed in prominent places throughout the building.

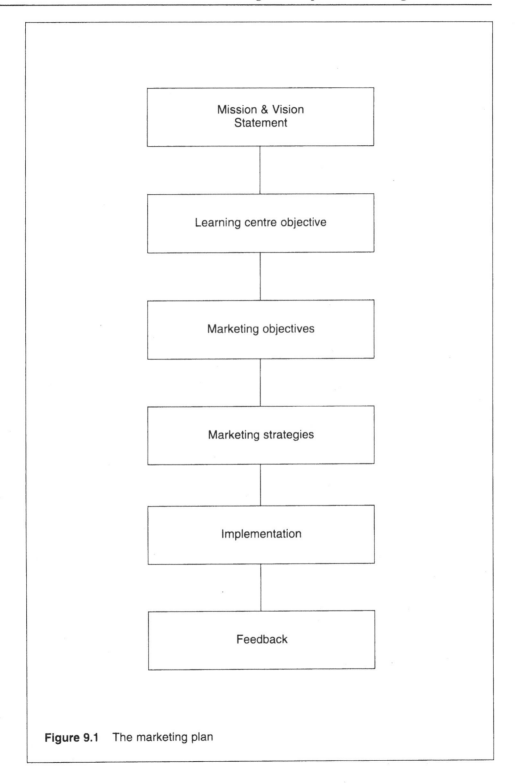

Figure 9.1   The marketing plan

Learning centre objectives

The mission and vision statement is followed by the corporate learning centre objectives. The objectives should be clearly stated, realistic and capable of measurement. They set down where the corporate learning centre would like to be in a few years time. It might be expressed in the form of targets of numbers of employees completing various training programmes to achieve business objectives over a defined period of time.

Where are you now?

The next step is the *position audit*. Where are you now, and what resources do you have? Look at your existing situation – the hardware and course programmes you have currently in the corporate learning centre. Make a list, and consider whether they are the best available and meet the present and proposed needs of the centre. Ideally, you should benchmark against the best of your competitors and the best currently available. It is always better to buy equipment with the more advanced specifications which are needed for multimedia applications. Similarly, it is often false economy to buy in cheap courseware. It might be cheap because it is out of date or about to be superseded by a new version.

Compare this with your objectives, and you will discover the gap between your present position and your desired position.

Marketing objectives

The marketing objectives for the corporate learning centre should be linked to individual training plans, section work programmes, business plans, and ultimately to the corporate plan. Marketing objectives can be expressed in terms of:

- persuading your existing customers to make more use of the centre
- developing new customers for your existing products
- developing new products for your existing customers
- developing new products for new customers.

In general, you should market benefits, not features. Features might include types of packages, media, equipment and tutorial support. The benefits might include:

- convenience and accessibility of open learning
- development of new skills, leading to greater job satisfaction and prospects for promotion
- acquisition of qualifications, leading to higher status and better job prospects

- more productive use of free time
- self-empowerment.

How to persuade existing customers to make more use of the centre

There are three basic options: you may encourage learners to move on to more intensive courses, or try new courses within the centre, or you may suggest that they make use of the loan service to benefit from programmes they can follow in their own time.

Finding new customers

Your starting point for new customers should be employees within the organization who have not yet visited the centre or used the material within it. Encouraging senior and middle managers to use the centre may help promote the centre to all staff, who will follow their lead.

Once the centre has been established, you may cast your net wider to include the families of employees or staff from other organizations or contractors. The decision to extend the centre's services beyond immediate employees should be measured against the centre's mission, vision and objectives, and bearing in mind any security, health and safety and copyright issues it will raise.

Club membership

Another idea might be to offer club membership of the centre, with an annual subscription. Benefits of membership would include use of the centre on payment of a small fee for each course studied there, a monthly or quarterly newsletter sent to subscribers, and advice on sources and the quality of open learning courseware. Advice on setting up a corporate learning centre would warrant separate negotiated fees. Club membership might help to spread the workload over the year, and at the same time earn revenue for the centre.

Consultancy

The corporate learning centre could be opened up as a training facility and consultancy service for overseas clients. Professional liability insurance may need to be taken out if you are offering a consultancy service to third parties, and once again, you should take this decision only if it accords with your mission, vision and objectives, and you are able to square the copyright issues involved.

New products and services

The centre might offer new services, such as access to the Internet or stocking new subjects that are currently topical and relevant to people's interests, lives and careers. Subjects of recreational interest and covering personal development could also be stocked. Facilities and opening hours might be improved to cater to the needs of customers. Longer opening hours might meet the needs of staff who are unable to use the service during normal working hours. Large companies may develop their own courseware and e-learning programmes, which could then be sold on to other organizations.

You may identify one of the barriers to the centre's use as gaps in your course material. If potential new customers indicate a need you cannot currently fill, explore the possibility of expanding your range to attract these new customers. Once they become centre users, you may encourage them to try other existing programmes.

New technology

Corporate learning centre courseware (and indeed hardware) quickly becomes outdated, and must be replaced by more current versions. This is standard practice with computer courseware producers and e-learning providers, who update their products frequently, and the co-ordinator should ensure that the latest version is being used.

Computer technology is moving ahead at an increasingly rapid rate. The CD-ROM/DVD software is more graphical and interactive, and thus takes up more computer memory space. There is an ongoing need to upgrade computer specifications in line with developments in courseware and Internet use. In practice, it is always better to err on the generous side when determining computer specifications, as upgrading may be more expensive or, in some instances, may not be possible. Personal computers should be depreciated over two years rather than four years if you wish to keep up with the best technology. Gordon Moore, founder of Intel Corporation, formulated Moore's Law, which states that every 18 months the processing power of computers doubles while costs stay constant.

Pricing and charging

The corporate learning centre will set a price for its service to meet its marketing and financial objectives. Pricing is a complex area, and the system chosen will depend on the objectives of the organization. The simplest pricing structure involves the addition of a mark-up to total costs, to cover any additional overheads and the desired level of profits. Price should have regard to local competition. Individual employees should not be charged for using the centre, but there may be a charge-out for departments.

Promotion

Promotion creates awareness and stimulates interest in the services of the centre. It involves advertising and techniques of publicity and personal selling. Brochures, posters, pocket diaries, pens and mouse mats with the corporate learning centre logo, bookmarkers, calendars, newsletters, e-mail and noticeboards are all used to advertise and keep the centre in the forefront of people's minds. Posters eventually merge into the background and thus lose their impact after some time, particularly if they are put on a general noticeboard competing with other items. Special promotions to entice employees to use the centre may occasionally be necessary. They could take the form of prizes or entry into draws for users of the centre. Another way of enticing people into the centre is to hold events or seminars there. Invite guest speakers along to talk about current issues, or encourage staff to use it for meetings or team talks during off-peak times.

Formal learning does not stop, as many people think, when you leave school or college. Marketing will remind you of this fact, and encourage you to constantly upgrade your knowledge and develop new skills as the need arises. As the saying goes: 'Use it or lose it.' There is evidence to suggest that the brains of those who challenge themselves intellectually continue to grow.

Customer database and mailing

With a personal computer, word-processing and database software, the learning centre co-ordinator has all the resources necessary for a direct marketing campaign. The learning management system will carry the details of the employees who have used the centre, and may also have access to the general personnel database on all employees of the company. This database can be used to target specific groups or individuals regarding new courseware or courses they have not done yet.

Displays and brand image

A special corporate learning centre display area should be considered. Review all posters frequently. The centre's logo should appear on screens when the computers are switched on. The corporate learning centre should have its own Website. Stationery should also be designed. This is all part of the process of creating an identifiable brand image.

Personal selling

Personal selling involves promoting the services of the centre to interested parties. Presentations may be designed to increase business and awareness, or to create goodwill and improve the prospects of custom in the future. Personal visits to managers will help co-ordinators to keep in touch with training needs, and demonstrate how open learning can be used to meet those needs. Actively encouraging managers to suggest new subject areas will improve commitment to the centre and take-up of courses. What better way to find out what managers want than by going and asking them?

Loans service

The co-ordinator must plan for the availability of the courseware, and in the case of the loan service for texts, audio, CDs and video, the distribution channel to be used. This might be the internal corporate postal system, the Post Office or special courier. Where there are several corporate learning centres in the company, then you could consider the possibility of networking. In the case of e-learning programmes, the Internet or intranet will be the distribution channel.

Information and feedback

Once you have established your strategy, draw up an action plan to record when certain activities will take place and who exactly is responsible for them. The action plan can be converted into a budget to control expenditure. A good learning management system will record course bookings, keep track of learning progress and completions, and produce monthly management control information. Actual costs can be compared with budgets on a monthly basis. Actual number of bookings can be compared with targets. Market research will result in feedback from users of the centre, and this should be used to improve services.

Corporate learning centre lifecycle

This cycle consists of four stages – *planning, introducing, embedding* and *sustaining.*

- **Planning:**
  - identifying training needs
  - winning the support of line management
  - hardware, software and telecommunications infrastructure
  - learning management system
  - e-learning providers
  - marketing plan
  - staffing
  - quality standards and criteria of effectiveness
  - budgeting.

- **Introducing:**
  - promoting the centre
  - facilitating learners
  - monitoring the effectiveness of media and courses
  - communicating with stakeholders.

- **Embedding:**
  - improving the service in response to stakeholder demands
  - integrating the centre with business needs and mainstream training
  - adding new centres in response to needs
  - weeding out and updating courses as necessary
  - demonstrating effectiveness as regards cost, value for money and contribution to business needs.

- **Sustaining:**
  - extending the centre's role in meeting training and business needs
  - evaluation and development
  - expansion, updating and replacement of course materials
  - ongoing marketing and sales promotion.

Service – a total quality management (TQM) approach

The best form of marketing is word of mouth. Clients appreciate an excellent service and remember a good experience, and will recommend the centre to their colleagues and superiors. The goodwill created will enhance and secure the centre's reputation. Total quality management means getting it right first time, and this should be the objective of the corporate learning centre. TQM means cost-effective, continuous improvement of the learning environment, the courseware, e-learning programmes and hardware resources, and the quality of the service. Quality must be monitored, feedback from learners obtained, shortcomings identified, and continuous improvement implemented. It is through TQM that the corporate learning centre will win friends and influence people. The British Association for Open Learning (BAOL) Quality Mark scheme allows learning centres to assess their operations against standards and best practice.

The whole philosophy of the corporate learning centre is to encourage people to learn and to go on learning throughout their careers. Any barriers that prevent them doing this should be eliminated. Learning should be made as easy as possible. The policies of the corporate learning centre should reflect this objective. The procedures for booking courses and using the centre should be as simple as possible.

Summary

The importance of a marketing plan was highlighted in this chapter. A systematic approach to marketing a corporate learning centre was suggested. Marketing should be thought through, and not left to chance. A good plan always starts with the mission and vision statement, and then works through to the objectives. Marketing objectives are about retaining existing customers and creating new ones. The marketing approach during the corporate learning centre's lifecycle was considered. The marketing mix strategies – a quality service, sales promotion and personal selling – will help you achieve your objectives.

10 The learner's guide to a corporate learning centre

Introduction

Corporate learning centres place much of the responsibility for self-development on the learners. The corporate learning centre co-ordinator should use every opportunity to help and support this process. You may reproduce the material in this chapter to supply to employees. Alternatively, you may develop your own 'user guide' by drawing on the material.

Considering the co-ordinator's perspective

Foresight and planning will ensure that your visit to the learning centre will have a successful outcome. Consider what you hope to learn, how your manager expects you to benefit, what the course is going to be like, how to benefit from the course, and what support systems are available in the company to help you. Support systems may include your manager, other learners, mentor, work colleagues – and, of course, the co-ordinator.

Put yourself in the co-ordinator's shoes. What preparation would you like learners to have done before they visit the centre, and what would you like them to do when they visit the centre? It should not need to be said, but manners and courtesy are important.

Consulting the guide

First obtain a copy of the users' guide to courses from the co-ordinator, or consult the intranet for the online guide. This is your map of the corporate learning centre. It will include the booking procedure, a map showing where the centre is located and how to get there, and the telephone number. The guide lists all courses. However, new courses are added continuously and some may be withdrawn, so ring your co-ordinator or consult the intranet to find out the up-to-date position. In the mean time, study the guide carefully. Courses may be categorized under subject area and within subject area under code, title, type – text, audio, CD, video, CD-ROM/DVD, e-learning – and duration. Before you begin, find out as much as you can about the course from other learners who have completed it. Remember, you may use the home loan service for audio, CDs, video and text. Armed with this information, you are now in a position to discuss your needs with the learning centre co-ordinator.

Scheduling visits

Visits to the centre will need to fit in with the demands of your work. The co-ordinator will try to balance your requirements against the capacity of the centre and the level of bookings. Demand will fluctuate at different times of the year, days of the week and hours of the day. Ask your co-ordinator when is the best time to book. The particular booth you want may have already been booked by another person, or the particular home loan course may have been loaned out. Remember to plan and book your requirements well in advance.

Reproduced from *How to Set Up and Manage a Corporate Learning Centre*, Samuel A. Malone, Gower, Aldershot.

Bookings

If booking by phone, refer to the users' guide for the exact title of the course and its code. The length of prior notice really depends on the level of demand on your learning centre, but 24 hours' notice might be considered a minimum requirement. Some facilities might be more in demand than others, for example CD-ROM/DVD-based courses on information technology, so more notice would be needed for them. Home loan courses in the personal development area may also be in big demand. Corporate needs such as special training initiatives may increase the demand in specific subjects.

Remember, it is good manners to let your co-ordinator know of cancellations well in advance, to ensure facilities are not tied up unnecessarily and other bookings can be accepted. Likewise, let the co-ordinator know if you change your mind regarding the course you want to study.

Setting personal objectives

The courses in the corporate learning centre should form part of the approach to your individual training needs and to your personal goals and ambitions. Personal development plans may have been drawn up by you in conjunction with your immediate supervisor or manager. There will be various ways of meeting your identified training needs, such as on-the-job and off-the-job training. Part of your off-the-job training will be met by attending in-company and outside training programmes. Some of your formal training needs may also be met by attending corporate learning centre courses, including Internet-based e-learning programmes, which may be more convenient and suitable for you than attending formal 'live' courses.

Your supervisor or manager should take into account the courses available in the corporate learning centre when agreeing your individual training plans. Unfortunately, this doesn't always happen. Staff attend courses outside the company at great expense even though an equivalent course is available in the local learning centre.

Setting objectives is one of the best ways to motivate yourself. Learning is a continuous process. When you have acquired one skill, there are always others that could prove useful in our job and career. Nothing stands still, and even existing knowledge and skills need to be updated and improved from time to time. Objectives should be measurable and bounded by a time constraint – that which can be done at any time is rarely done at all. So a time plan is most important.

Because of demands on your time and the way in which we learn, the 'little and often' approach is more effective than spending many hours at the centre in one go. With three hours devoted to open learning over the

Reproduced from *How to Set Up and Manage a Corporate Learning Centre*, Samuel A. Malone, Gower, Aldershot.

course of a week, you could acquire many skills over a period of a few months. You need persistence and commitment to be successful in open learning. Enlist the help of the co-ordinator when setting your objectives and drawing up your plans to achieve them. The fact that a third party knows about your plans will help you stick to your commitments.

Choosing courses

Some courses might be of direct benefit to you, in that you can apply them immediately to your work. Other courses might be of a development nature. They will contribute to your long-term development, and prepare you for more demanding work or more responsible positions in the future. Self-development courses may help you as a person to improve your lot in life. Of course, they may also indirectly benefit your working life, although this is not the prime purpose. Key and match the course to your individual identified training needs. Agree the time of attendance with your immediate supervisor or manager.

Skills-based courses, such as those on information technology, are usually the most suitable to the corporate learning centre approach. 'Soft' skills courses, such as interpersonal relations, public speaking and inter-group dynamics, are more appropriate to a 'live' programme with participants and a course facilitator. However, the theory and knowledge content of these subjects can be learned quite effectively in a corporate learning centre. This would suggest that you use the corporate learning centre before attending these 'soft' skills courses, and after them to refresh the knowledge, and that this should be formally incorporated as part of these programmes. This is the blended learning approach in action.

Beginning with the basics

You may want to take notes while taking part in the course, so make sure to bring a notebook and pen with you. Most courses have introductory skills sections. If you are unfamiliar with the keyboard, why not take a keyboard skills course before you tackle the more sophisticated programmes, or a PC familiarization course such as the ECDL? If you are unfamiliar with the Internet, why not take the Internet familiarization programme? The co-ordinator will advise you. Remember, most of us crawl before we walk, and it is a good idea to learn the fundamentals before you attempt the more difficult programmes.

Learning outside the centre

Corporate learning centre courses offer only one way to meet your

Reproduced from *How to Set Up and Manage a Corporate Learning Centre*, Samuel A. Malone, Gower, Aldershot.

identified training needs. Other ways include on-the-job and off-the-job training. On-the-job training might include job rotation, project work, negotiations, committee work and making presentations to other employees. You can, of course, use the facilities of the corporate learning centre to brush up on these areas as necessary.

Off-the-job training might include doing formal professional or certificate, diploma, degree or postgraduate courses. Some colleges are offering these as Internet-based e-learning programmes. Many of the courses in the corporate learning centre will prove of benefit to your formal studies. Ask the co-ordinator to help you draw up a formal plan to integrate your studies with the open learning courses available. You can also use the loan service and audio, CDs, video and text-based courses at home, or in the case of audio/CD, while commuting.

Recording your progress

The co-ordinator, through the learning management system, will keep a record of your attendance at corporate learning centre courses, which in turn may be linked to the personal management information system and your personal records. If this is the case, the co-ordinator will explain the system, and how it works. In addition, most of the computer-based training programmes keep records of your progress during the course. As part of your personal development plan, you should keep your own formal record of the courses you have attended in the corporate learning centre, including their code, description and duration of the course. Record how you applied the course to the job, and how the work situation benefited as a result. You may choose to involve your mentor or your boss in this process. The emphasis of the centre is on your learning and development, so it remains a personal issue for you.

Your record of courses attended will support any application for internal promotion. The interview panel may ask you about the courses, and how you have applied them to your work situation. It is a sign of commitment to the company's goals and to your own personal development if you have a good record of attending corporate learning centre courses, and it will not go unnoticed at an interview. A well-maintained record of courses and their outcome and application will provide any future employer with evidence of skills and motivation.

Using the co-ordinator

The co-ordinator has a fund of knowledge about the corporate learning centre courses available, and will be only too delighted to share it with you, but make sure that the timing is right. There are busy days of the week and hours of the day when the co-ordinator may not have the time

Reproduced from *How to Set Up and Manage a Corporate Learning Centre*, Samuel A. Malone, Gower, Aldershot.

to be as helpful as he or she might wish. Use your common sense. Ask the best time to consult about the courses, and make an appropriate appointment. This will help the co-ordinator to give you the attention you deserve. When booking your course by phone, be organized. Plan your calls. Write down what you need to find out, and keep the call short and to the point. Clients who haven't organized their thoughts in advance waste their own time and that of the co-ordinator.

Feedback to your manager

Keep your manager informed about the courses you are studying in the corporate learning centre, and it will help you to win approval. Before each course, discuss it with your manager, and how it fits in with your personnel development plan, and the needs of the department or section. After attending the course, discuss the benefits of the programme with the manager, and how the work of the department or section is going to improve as a result of your application. Providing continuous feedback to your manager will reinforce the benefits of your learning and development, and provide you with help and advice in return.

Feedback to the co-ordinator

The co-ordinator will help you choose the most appropriate course and identify other training suitable to your needs when you are ready to pursue more advanced courses or different programmes. If you consult your co-ordinator when you are about to attend an external course, he or she may be able to suggest a pre-course familiarizer which will help you learn more effectively on the 'live' programme. Learning centre courses may also be used to revise and reinforce knowledge and skills acquired on 'live' courses. Your feedback and suggestions will help the co-ordinator to develop the centre's service and identify and purchase new courses or source new e-learning programmes.

Personal housekeeping

At the centre, keep your work area tidy. When you are finished, put your courseware away in the presses, or give it back to the co-ordinator. Return the screen to the opening menu ready for the next learner. Remove your personal belongings. A little thought will help not just the co-ordinator, but other learners as well. Remember, the next learner is your internal customer – so leave the booth in the condition you would like to have it for yourself. Fill out any course evaluation forms, and hand them to the co-ordinator before you leave. If you want to book in for more

Reproduced from *How to Set Up and Manage a Corporate Learning Centre*, Samuel A. Malone, Gower, Aldershot.

sessions during the rest of the week, now might be a good opportunity to do so.

Summary

Preparation is the key to success. Getting the most from corporate learning centre courses means planning and thinking ahead. Make the most of your visit by paying attention to the following points:

- Schedule your visits with regard to the work situation and the demands on the learning centre.
- Book your course requirements in advance.
- Set yourself objectives, and draw up a time plan.
- Choose courses in line with your personal development plan, and agree these with your manager.
- Use the centre as part of your overall training and development plan.
- Keep a record of completed courses.
- Use the co-ordinator's experience to your advantage.
- Inform your manager about your plans and progress.
- Inform your co-ordinator about all your training plans.
- Keep your work area tidy while at the centre.

Reproduced from *How to Set Up and Manage a Corporate Learning Centre*, Samuel A. Malone, Gower, Aldershot.

11 Conclusions and recommendations

24 Questions for planning a centre

The following questions are designed to help you reflect on your learning centre strategy:

1. What is the likely market for your centre?

2. What topics will it cover?

3. What types of courseware should it contain, and what e-learning programmes should it subscribe to?

4. How and where will you source courseware?

5. What sort of media should it have?

6. Where will it be located?

7. How should it be equipped, furnished and laid out?

8. Who are the suppliers of equipment?

9. What is the timetable for setup?

10. What is the centre's mission, vision and objectives?

11. What are the forces which either help or hinder the corporate learning centre?

12. How will it integrate with 'live' training programmes?

13. What will be the staffing arrangements?

14. How much support will the company give staff to use the corporate learning centre?

15. What training will the co-ordinator require?

16. What size of budget will be needed for setting up and running the centre?

17. In the case of multiple sites, should they be standalone or networked?

18. Will the centre be treated as a profit centre, or absorbed as an overhead?

19. How will you identify training needs?

20. How will you evaluate courseware?

21. How will you advertise and promote the learning centre?

22. How will you attract new corporate learning centre customers in the short, medium and long term?

23. How will you monitor the operation of the corporate learning centre and establish whether or not it is a success?

24. How will you operate the stock and loans management system for audio, CD, video and text-based courses?

The future

The accessibility, flexibility and convenience of corporate learning centres should ensure a bright future in meeting identified training and development needs. The sense of isolation and lack of social interaction will mean they will never completely replace traditional training, but will complement it and enrich it. Some experts predict a convergence of e-learning, performance management, knowledge management and other types of training.

Most workers in Europe have access to a PC or computer terminal. This raises the possibility of just-in-time training (JITT), where employees could access training courseware and knowledge as and when they need it. Knowledge management systems already facilitate this process. Using a local area network (LAN), PCs in the same building can be linked together. PCs which are distributed over wider geographical areas can be linked together using a national or an international wide area network (WAN). Training can now be delivered direct to the learner's own PC. Through the Internet, PCs are linked globally. However, the average workplace does not provide a conducive learning environment, hence the need for corporate learning centres. For example, Sloman (2001) found that British Airways' employees preferred discrete workstations. The BA study showed that telephones, e-mail and interruptions by other staff were a major distraction to learning.

The television set will be important in the learning centre of the future. With cable link, the technology is already in place. Subscription learning channels could incorporate a menu for users to interrogate a course programme of their choice. With developments in technology, the PC can also double as a TV. Currently there are PCs on sale which can do this. The future penetration of the domestic market with PC/TVs means that there will be the nucleus of a corporate learning centre in each household. Some TVs can also be used for Internet access, as can mobile phones. The use of wireless technology in mobile phones for learning is known as m-learning. This is the ultimate facility for just-in-time learning.

The miniaturization of computers such as hand-held ones, and the improved functionality of mobile phone with Internet access offer a glimpse of the future. The technology is there. It is now a question of creating the demand for such services. Microsoft's goals is to be able to deliver near-broadcast quality video content on PCs. In the future, the company intranet will be the most important vehicle for the delivery of training. Management guru Peter F. Drucker predicts traditional residential higher education will be obsolete within thirty years.

Continuous marketing

To maintain interest and a high rate of usage in a corporate learning centre, continuous marketing is a key part of the success formula. In addition, existing packages must be updated and new programmes purchased. The best of e-learning programmes should be accessible from the centre. These must be vetted carefully by subject matter experts for relevance and quality. Nothing does more damage to a corporate learning centre's image than poor-quality courses. To attract custom, self-development and recreational packages should also be stocked. Marketing research using a questionnaire is needed on an annual or more frequent basis to keep in touch with the views and needs of the centre's users.

Management support

A corporate learning centre cannot be successful without the active support of top management, from the chief executive down. Senior managers, as role models and as an expression of their active support and commitment, should use the centre themselves, if only on an occasional basis. If the chief executive were to use the centre even infrequently, it would work wonders for bookings. Leadership should be by example.

Attendance at corporate learning centre courses should be an issue at interviews for internal positions, and should be part of the appraisal and reward system. If word gets around that it helps career progression, ambitious people will be very eager to pursue corporate learning centre courses.

Managers should actively encourage their staff to use the corporate learning centre to meet individual training needs and for personal development. Open learning should be incorporated into the culture of the company. Allowance for corporate learning centre usage should be an integral part of work programmes, individual training plans and budgets. Usage should be reviewed by managers each month.

Managers should allocate at least two hours to each staff member for this purpose. In practice, some staff complain that they are unable to take part in corporate learning centre courses because of pressure of work, and that managers do not encourage them to use its service. For job-related courses, as much time as is practicable should be allowed. If an employee needs 20 hours for a particular course, then the manager should schedule this over a number of weeks.

Outside working hours

The take-up of courses in the corporate learning centre outside normal working hours is usually sporadic. This is understandable, since people have other lives to lead outside their work. Some type of monetary incentive may be necessary to improve usage outside working hours. Staff might be encouraged to use the 'twilight' hours between 4 p.m. and 7 p.m., immediately after work. This saves people the trouble of going home and coming back again. Weekends may also be targeted.

Organizational databases

In the future, greater use will be made of information technology and knowledge management systems to provide facilities for learning and to provide information to design in-house customized courses. Dorrell (1993) supports this view. She reckons organizations will have databases with information on:

- company background
- organization charts, where necessary
- company culture and mission statements
- departmental/divisional responsibilities
- individual responsibilities, and how these relate to each other
- whole-organization job descriptions.

Most large organizations have this information already on file. These courses could be designed using a variety of media, including print, audio, CD, video, CD-ROM/DVD and the Internet. Thus, induction courses could be run in the corporate learning centre. New employees can help themselves to this information as needed, and assimilate it more quickly and more effectively. Most large companies are now developing knowledge management systems so that corporate knowledge can be recorded, codified and accessed in small chunks as and when required, facilitating just-in-time learning.

Corporate learning centre management

The success or failure of a corporate learning centre depends very much on the calibre, commitment and dedication of the co-ordinator and local management. The enthusiasm of line management and staff is also a prerequisite. Co-ordinators need excellent customer relations and information technology skills, while managers need to have a special interest in educational technology, marketing and learning and the training and development of staff.

Functionally, the corporate learning centres could be part of Training and Development or under the control of the local personnel manager or line manager. If the company has a corporate library, maybe the library might be the best place to site the learning centre, as it is a complementary service. However, its location and management will depend on the particular culture and circumstances of the company. In a large multi-site organization, corporate learning centres should be networked rather than standalone entities.

Summary

Corporate learning centres play a prominent role in the delivery of high-quality training programmes within many companies. To be successful, six basic criteria must be met:

1. Appropriate hardware and accommodation resources must be provided.
2. A wide range of high-quality courseware driven by training and business needs must be stocked in the corporate learning centre.
3. Quality e-learning programmes must be subscribed to.
4. The centre must be staffed by a capable full-time co-ordinator.
5. The centre must be supported by management and staff, and be part of the appraisal and salary review process.
6. The centre must be marketed actively.

Appendix:
Information sources

1. Other open learning centres

2. The *Open Learning Directory* lists a wide range of open learning materials, and is available from Heinemann Publishers, Customer Services Department, PO Box 283, Oxon. Ox2 8RU. Tel. 01865 310366

3. British Association for Open Learning, Suite No. 16, Pixmoor House, Pixmoor Avenue, Letchworth, Herts. SG6 1JG. Tel. 0146 485588

4. Training managers in other companies. Consult the CIPD Register for members.

5. <http://www.learningcircuits.org>

6. <http://www.elearningzone.co.uk>

7. <http://www.elearningmag.com>

8. <http://www.e-learningprofessional.com>

Bibliography

Austin, Mary B. 1992. 'CBT From Scratch – Building a Computer Based Training Department', *Tech Trends*, vol. 37, pp.9–11.

Bajtelmit, John W. 1990. 'Study Methods in Distance Education: A Summary of Five Research Studies'. *Contemporary Issues in American Distance Education*, ed. Michael G. Moore, Pergamon Press, Oxford, pp.181–91.

Bates, Tony. 1988. 'Delivery and New Technology', *Open Learning in Transition; An Agenda for Action*, ed. Nigel Paine, National Extension College, Cambridge, pp.364–77.

Birchall, D. 1990. 'Third Generation Distance Learning', *Journal of European Industrial Training*, vol. 14, 7, pp.17–20.

Boulding, T. 1989. 'Long-distance learning', *Personnel Management*, vol. 21, 1, pp.31–2.

Chute, Alan G., Balthazar, Lee B. and Poston, Carol O. 1990. 'Learning from Teletraining: What AT & T Research Says', *Contemporary Issues in American Education*, ed. Michael G. Moore, Pergamon Press, Oxford, pp.260–275.

Coldeway, Dan O. 1982. 'What Does Educational Psychology Tell Us About the Adult Learner at a Distance?', *Learning at a Distance: A World Perspective*, ed. John S. Daniel, Martha A. Stroud and John R. Thompson, Athabasca University/International Correspondence Education, Edmonton, pp.90–3.

Crawley, Richard. 1988. 'Flexible Training Systems: Breaking the Mould of Training in Britain', *Open Learning in Transition; An Agenda for Action*, ed. Nigel Paine, National Extension College, Cambridge, pp.326–36.

Daniel, John. 1988. 'The Worlds of Open Learning', *Open Learning in Transition: An Agenda for Action*, ed. Nigel Paine, National Extension College, Cambridge, pp.126–36.

Davies, Mike. 2001. 'Implementing E-learning Strategies and Advice', *Training Journal*, August.

Davies, W. J. K. 1989. *Open and Flexible Learning Centres*, National College for Educational Technology, London.

Dillich, Sandra. 2000. 'Corporate Universities: More companies are Creating Their Own Corporate Universities in Order to Train Employees', *Computing Canada*, 4 August.

Dobson, Roger. 1988. 'Tomorrow's Training Today', *Open Learning in Transition: An Agenda for Action*, ed. Nigel Paine, National Extension College, Cambridge, pp.319–25.

Dorrell, Julia. 1993. *Resource-based Learning: Using Open and Flexible Learning Resources for Continuous Development*, McGraw-Hill Training Series, London.

Draper, James A. 1982. 'Adult Education: A Perspective for the Eighties', *Learning at a Distance: A World Perspective*, ed. John S. Daniel, Martha A. Stroud and John R. Thompson, Athabasca University/International Council for Correspondence Education, Edmonton, pp.43–6.

Dunn, Patrick. 2001. 'Has E-learning Truly Arrived in Europe?', *Training Journal*, October.

Dwyer, Frank M. 1990. 'Enhancing the Effectiveness of Distance Education: A Proposed Research Agenda', *Contemporary Issues in American Distance Education*, ed. Michael G. Moore, Pergamon Press, Oxford, pp.221–9.

Enright, Greg. 2002. 'Going the Distance', *Computer Dealer News*, 17 September.

Fahy, Michael. 1989. 'Long Distance Learning', *Network Work*, vol. 6, 48, pp.39–40.

Florina, Barbara M. 1990. 'Delivery Systems for Distance Education: Focus on Computer Conferencing', *Contemporary Issues in American Education*, ed. Michael G. Moore. Pergamon Press, Oxford, pp.277–89.

Forlenza, D. 1995. 'Computer-based Training', *Professional Safety*, May, vol. 40, 5, pp.28–9.

Forsythe, Kathleen. 1982. 'Learning to Learn', *Learning at a Distance: A World Perspective*, ed. John S. Daniel, Martha A. Stroud and John R. Thompson. Athabasca University/International Council for Correspondence Education, Edmonton, pp.219–21.

Franchi, Jorge. 1992. 'CBT or IVD? – That's the Question', *Tech Trends*, vol. 37, Part 2, pp.27–30.

Freathy, Paul. 1991. 'Distance Learning and the Distributive Trades: Stirling's MBA', *Journal of European Industrial Training*, vol. 15, 4, pp.21–4.

Freeman, Richard, 1982. 'Flexistudy', *Learning at a Distance: A World Perspective*, ed. John S. Daniel, Martha A. Stroud and John R. Thomson,

Athabasca University/International Council for Correspondence Education, Edmonton, pp.162–5.

Fricker, John. 1988. 'Open Learning – What's in it for Business?', *Open Learning in Transition: An Agenda for Action*, ed. Nigel Paine, National Extension College, Cambridge, pp.337–47.

Galagan, Patricia A. 2001. 'Mission E-possible: The Cisco E-learning Story', *Training and Development*, February.

Ganger, Ralph. E. 1994. 'Training: Computer-based', *Personnel Journal*, November, pp.1–5.

Geisman, Julia. 2001. 'If You Build It, Will They Come? Overcoming Human Obstacles to E-Learning', *ASTD Learning Circuits*, March.

Gibson, Chere Campell. 1990. 'Learners and Learning: A Discussion of Selected Research', *Contemporary Issues in American Distance Education*, ed. Michael G. Moore. Pergamon Press, Oxford, pp.121–33.

Hall, Brandon, 2001, 'Six Steps to Developing a Successful E-learning Initiative: Excerpts from the E-learning Guidebook', *The ASTD E-learning Handbook: Best Practices, Strategies, and Case Studies for an Emerging Field*, ed. Allison Rossett, McGraw-Hill, New York.

Hall, Brandon. 2002. 'Brandon Hall: Sharing an Experience', *Training Journal*, May.

Handy, Charles. 1988. 'The New Management', *Open Learning in Transition: An Agenda for Action*, ed. Nigel Paine, National Extension College, Cambridge, pp.116–25.

Harper, Karl. 1993. 'Why Flexible Learning?', *Banking World*, vol. 11, 8, pp.45–6.

Harris, Jeff. 2002. 'An Introduction to Authoring Tools', *ASTD Learning Circuits*, March.

Hills, Howard. 2002. 'The Shape of the E-learning Marketplace: Its Products, Services and Customers', *Training Journal*, February.

Islam, Kaliym. 2002. 'Is E-learning Floundering?', *e-learning magazine*, May.

Johnston, Rita. 1993. 'The Role of Distance Learning in Professional Development', *Management Services*, vol. 37, 4, pp.24–6.

Jones, Chris. 1998. 'The World Comes to Milton Keynes', *New Statesman*, 13 November.

Kattackal, R. 1994. 'Plugging in to computer based training', *Internal Auditor*, December, vol. 51, 6, pp.32–6.

Kay, Alan S. 1995. 'The Business Case for Multi-media', *Datamation*, June, vol. 41, 11, pp. 55–6.

Kearsley, Dr Michael A. 2002. 'Web-based Training: A View of the Future', *Training Journal*, May.

Keegan, Desmond. 1990. *Foundations of Distance Education*, 2nd edn, Routledge, London and New York, pp.3–45 and 183–209.

Lamb, John. 2002. 'Moving Inside the Virtual Classroom', *Understanding E-learning*, March.

Moshinskie, Jim. 2001. 'How to Keep E-learners from E-scaping', *The*

ASTD E-Learning Handbook, ed. Allison Rossett, McGraw-Hill, New York.

Lavitt, Michael O. 1995. 'Multimedia System Provides Training in Aircraft ID', *Aviation Week and Space Technology*, January, vol. 142, 2, p.54.

Lewis, Roger. 1988. 'Open Learning – The Future', *Open Learning in Transition: An Agenda for Action*, ed. Nigel Paine. National Extension College, Cambridge, pp.175–89.

Linstead, Stephen. 1990. 'Developing Management Meta-competence: Can Distance Learning Help?', *Journal of European Industrial Training*, vol. 14, 6, p.17–27.

Littlefield, David. 1994. 'Opening Learning by PC or Paper?', *Personnel Management*, September, vol. 26, p.55.

Malone, Samuel. 2000. *Learning Skills for Managers*, Oaktree Press, Dublin.

Markowitz Jr, Harold. 1990. 'Continuing Professional Development in Distance Education', *Contemporary Issues in American Distance Education*, ed. Michael G. Moore. Pergamon Press, Oxford, pp.58–66.

Martin, Peter L. 2001. 'E-finance (Status of E-learning Corporate Sector)', *Training and Development*, July.

Masie, Elliott. 2002a. 'Creating a Culture of Learning', *e-learning magazine*, 1 February.

Masie, Elliott. 2002b. 'Infusing E-learning: Strategies for acceptance', *e-learning magazine*, 1 March.

Murray, P. 1993. 'Quality Learning, A Personal View, from a Fan of Open Learning', *BACIE*, January, vol. 93, 1, pp.8–9.

Oates, David. 1990. 'Small Business: Switched on to Distance Learning', *Director*, vol. 43, 12, p.127.

Pope, Scott. 2002. 'Form a Successful Strategy', *e-learning magazine*, 1 February.

Prickett, Ruth. 2002. 'A Second Byte', *CIMA Insider*, July/August.

Richardson, Michael. 1988. 'The National Extension College and the Open University – A Comparison of Two National Institutions', *Open Learning in Transition: An Agenda for Action*, ed. Nigel Paine, National Extension College, Cambridge, pp.57–69.

Rossenberg, J. Marc. 2001, 'The Four Cs of Success: Culture, Champions, Communication, and Change', *The ASTD E-Learning Handbook: Best Practices, Strategies, and Case Studies for an Emerging Field*, ed. Allison Rossett, McGraw-Hill, New York.

Rossett, Allison. 2002. *The ASTD E-learning Handbook: Best Practices, Strategies, and Case Studies for an Emerging Field*, McGraw-Hill. New York.

Shepherd, Clive. 2001a. 'Games E-learners Play', *e-Learning Professional*, 1 March.

Shepherd, Clive. 2001b. 'Seeing it Through', *e-Learning Professional*, 1 June.

Shlechter T. M. 1990. 'The Relative Instructional Efficiency of Small Group Computer Based Training', *Journal of Educational Computing Research*, vol. 6, 3, pp.329–41.

Singer, Karen. 2000. 'Distance-learning Ventures Propel Top Universities into Four Profit Sector', *Matrix: The Magazine for Leaders in Education*, November–December.

Skyrme, David. 2001. 'E-learning: Which Side of the Coin?', *Entovation International News*, December, No. 56.

Sloman, Martyn. 2001. *The E-learning Revolution – From Propositions to Action*, Chartered Institute of Personnel and Development, London.

Stephenson, Stanley D. 1992. 'The Role of the Instructor in Computer-based Training', *Performance & Instruction*, August, vol. 31, 7, pp.23–6.

Temple, Hilary. 1988. 'Open Learning in a Changing Climate', *Open Learning in Transition; An Agenda for Action*, ed. Nigel Paine, National Extension College, Cambridge, pp.201–11.

Thorpe, Mary. 1993. *Evaluating Open and Distance Learning*, Longman, Harlow.

Tuckett, Alan. 1988. 'Open Learning and the Education of Adults', *Open Learning in Transition: An Agenda for Action*, ed. Nigel Paine, National Extension College, Cambridge, pp.156–71.

Van den Brande, Lieve. 1993. *Flexible and Distance Learning*, John Wiley & Sons, New York, pp.1–34 and 233–8.

Vaughan Frazee, Rebecca, 2001. 'Technology Adoption: Bring Along the Latecomers', *The ASTD E-learning Handbook: Best Practices, Strategies, and Case Studies for an Emerging Field*, ed. Allison Rossett, McGraw-Hill, New York.

Waniewiczz, Ignacy. 1982. 'The Adult Learners: Who are They, Why and Where do They Learn?', *Learning at a Distance: A World Perspective*, ed. John S. Daniel, Martha A. Stroud and John R. Thompson, Athabasca University/International Council for Correspondence Education, Edmonton, pp.87–9.

Waterhouse, Philip. 1990. *Flexible Learning*, Network Educational Press, Bath.

Wedemeyer, Charles A. 1981. *Learning at the Back Door*, University of Wisconsin Press, Wisconsin and London, pp.47–73.

Williams, Shirley. 1988. 'Education and the Information Revolution', *Open Learning in Transition: An Agenda for Action*, ed. Nigel Paine, National Extension College, Cambridge, pp.81–91.

Wilson, David. 2001. 'The Economics of E-learning', *Training Journal*, May.

Index